Romantik
Journal for the Study of Romanticisms

Editors
Gísli Magnússon (University of Iceland), Benedikt Hjartarson (University of Iceland), Thor J. Mednick (University of Toledo), Lis Møller (Aarhus University), Elisabeth Oxfeldt (University of Oslo), Anna Lena Sandberg (University of Copenhagen), and Kim Simonsen (University of Amsterdam)

Advisory Board
Charles Armstrong (University of Bergen), Jacob Bøggild (University of Southern Denmark, Odense), David Fairer (University of Leeds), Karin Hoff (Georg-August-Universität Göttingen), Stephan Michael Schröder (University of Cologne), David Jackson (University of Leeds), Christoph Bode (LMU Munich), Carmen Casaliggi (Cardiff Metropolitan University), Gunilla Hermansson (University of Gothernburg), Knut Ljøgodt (Nordic Institute of Art, Oslo), Paula Henrikson (Uppsala University), Dorthe Jørgensen (University of Aarhus), and Joep Leerssen (University of Amsterdam)

Romantik
Journal for the Study of Romanticisms

Volume 09|2020

V&R unipress

Contents

Foreword 7

Articles

Peter Svare Valeur (The University of Bergen)
'What is This Strange Language?' Reflections on The Barbaric in
Jean-Jacques Rousseau and François-René De Chateaubriand 13

Adrian Mioc (University of Western Ontario, Canada)
Romantic Theories of Life: Coleridge and Shelley 33

Jørgen Huggler (Aarhus University)
Democracy, General Will, and Political Formation. Friedrich Schlegel's
Critique and Reconstruction of the Concept of 'Republicanism' 59

Louis Marvick (University of Nevada, Reno) /
Andrew Kent-Marvick (Southern Utah University)
Representing the Vortex: Delacroix's Critique of Poe's Sublime 75

Victoria Ferentinou (University of Ioannina)
Re-enchanting Art in Theory and Practice: Symbolism in Greece and
Frixos Aristeus 97

PhD Projects

Tim van Gerven (University of Amsterdam)
Scandinavism: Wiring Nationalism in the North 125

Katrine Wonge Lohmann (University of Copenhagen)
The Local Gothic 131

Review

Karen Klitgaard Povlsen
Friederike Brun, Weltbürgerin in der Zeitenwende. Ed. by Kerstin Gräfin
von Schwerin 137

About the Authors 141

Foreword

One of the ways to understand the *continuity* of romantic thought from 1780 and onward is to consider it as an attempt to re-enchant the world, which was disenchanted during the age of Enlightenment. Just to give one example: In the poem *Guldhornene* [*The Golden Horns*] (1803) by the Danish romantic poet Adam Oehlenschläger, the difference between the two world views is symbolized by two modes of perception: the rational perception of the golden horns as historical cultic artifacts and the romantic mode of perception that reinstates the divine dimension of the horns, symbolizing the re-enchantment of reality. Romanticism responded to a rational and one-sided scientific world view that – according to the romantics – threw the spiritual baby out with the bathwater of organized religion. The re-enchantment was, in other words, not a return to traditional religion, but rather mirrored elements from the current of modern esotericism. The romantic sacralization of art thereby became the prototypical response to a cold and meaningless cosmos, and this romantic figure of re-enchantment where the artwork is endowed with the aura and inexhaustibility that formerly belonged to religious artifacts. Despite his cosmic pessimism, Schopenhauer would continue this exact feature of romanticism, when he interpreted the contemplation of music and art, as the only way of redeeming us from the hell of the enslaved will. After the era of romanticism, the dialectics between disenchantment and re-enchantment became increasingly complicated. On the one hand, positivism heralded a new era of disenchantment, which manifested as realism and naturalism in literature and art. On the other hand, the programme of re-enchantment was prevalent in symbolism in the late 19th century and in the beginning of the 20th century. As in the era of romanticism, the symbolist poet assumed the role of *poeta vates*. Here we could mention Rainer Maria Rilke, who, in his opus magnum *The Sonnets to Orpheus* (1922) introduced Orpheus as a symbol of re-enchantment. In an era of disenchantment, materialism, industrialization, alienation and loss of meaning, the god of art emerged as an ideal figure showing ways to resacralize life through art and a holistic world view where the visible and invisible dimensions of the cosmos were in balance. But also later in the 20th century, we see many examples of re-enchantment, among others in modernism, avant-garde and magical realism. Franz Kafka, Jorge Luis Borges, Karen Blixen (Isaak Dinesen), and Gabriel García Márquez are just a few of the authors belonging to the modernism of re-enchantment. In the arts, Kandinsky is the most prominent aesthetic example of spiritual modernity – using visionary mimesis as a means of experimentation and re-enchantment. And, in 21st century posthumanism, ecology, and philosophy of nature are currents that seem to favour re-enchantment of nature as an alternative to instrumental rationality. This continuity shows us that ever since the historical current of romanticism, re-enchantment has been a culture-critical strategy, which has stayed relevant to authors, artists, and philosophers to this day.

* * *

For the past eight years, Robert Rix has been the editor-in-chief of *Romantik – Journal for the Study of Romanticisms.* During this period, *Romantik* established itself as an important journal for romanticism, not only in the Nordic countries, but on a wider international scale. A significant change took place as the journal shifted from Aarhus Universitets Forlag to Vandenhoeck & Ruprecht unipress in 2017. This – and its open source accessibility in Google Books – meant that the journal reached a greater and more international readership. Robert Rix has now decided to pass the baton to Prof. Gísli Magnússon from the University of Iceland. This has also led to changes in the editorial board where Prof. Benedikt Hjartarson (University of Iceland) and Dr. Kim Simonsen (University of Amsterdam) are new members of the editorial board. Dr. Lis Møller, Dr. Thor Mednik, Prof. Elisabeth Oxfeldt and Dr. Anna Lena Sandberg continue as members of the editorial board. Prof. Dorthe Jørgensen (University of Aarhus) and Prof. Joep Leerssen (University of Amsterdam) are new members of the advisory board.

The new editorial board will follow a twofold strategy: As hitherto, the journal is interested in all Nordic and European romanticisms. In this regard, our two boards are strengthened by the addition of Kim Simonsen and Joep Leerssen from the University of Amsterdam.[1] However, the new editorial board intends to widen the scope of the journal to encompass later expressions of romantic thought. Gísli Magnússon specializes in the continuity of romantic modes of thought until today. In his scholarship, he has e.g. shown the continuity of romantic ideas in the late-symbolist works of Rainer Maria Rilke via esotericism.

---

1 Joep Leerssen is well known for his *Encyclopedia of Romantic Nationalism in Europe* which is an ambitious collaborative research project involving hundreds of scholars. The result is accessible as open source on the internet (https://ernie.uva.nl/) and in book form in two volumes published by Amsterdam University Press.

And, recently he published an article on how the aesthetics of epiphany in the *My Struggle*-hexalogy (2009-2011) by Norwegian author Karl-Ove Knausgård is heavily influenced by romanticism. Benedikt Hjartarson is an expert on the avant-garde and the continuity of romantic thought in this current. New member of the advisory board Dorthe Jørgensen has also explored what she calls "the romantic-modern". According to her philosophical aesthetics, the figure of re-enchantment is still relevant to art and literature in the 20th and 21st century. In other words, *Romantik* will increasingly include currents after romanticism that aim at a re-enchantment of reality and a sacralization of art.

The renewal of *Romantik* will, however, be an evolution rather than a revolution. Most of the articles in the ninth issue of *Romantik* deal with the Romantic period in the strict sense; one article, however, demonstrates the relevance of the romantic idea of re-enchantment to symbolism. Two shorter articles describe ongoing PhD-projects; here we gain insight into the research interests of the coming generation of romanticism scholars. And finally, Karen Klitgaard Povlsen writes a review on the biography on the romantic cosmopolitan Friederike Brun by Kerstin Gräfin von Schwerin.

In the first article "Quel est ce langage étranger? Imaginations of the Barbaric in Jean-Jacques Rousseau and François-René de Chateaubriand", Peter Valeur examines the figure of the barbarian and barbarism in central works by these influential French thinkers. According to Valeur, Rousseau and Chateaubriand – despite living in different epochs – both saw the idea of barbarism as a means of challenging Enlightenment optimism. But whereas Rousseau embraced barbarism and violence as potentially emancipatory, Chateaubriand, the romantic, adhered to a more fatalist and nostalgic view.

In the article "Romantic Theories of Life: Coleridge and Shelley" Adrian Mioc juxtaposes two texts: Coleridge's *The Theory of Life* (1818) and Shelley's fragment *On Life* (1819; 1832). Mioc demonstrates how the texts relate to the scientific and philosophical discourse of the romantic era, and he detects both similarities and differences in their view of life and vitality. By delving into the intricacies and complexities of these theoretical works by two great romantic poets and thinkers, we learn about their view of wholeness, imagination, and divinity, mind, and life.

In the article "Democracy, General Will and Political Formation. Friedrich Schlegel's Critique and Reconstruction of the Concept of 'Republicanism'", Jørgen Huggler explores aspects of romantic philosophical thinking in a German context. Kant's treatise *Zum ewigen Frieden* [*Toward Perpetual Peace*], was widely read and translated into many languages shortly after its publication. Among the readers was Friedrich Schlegel who criticized Kant's distinction between republicanism and democracy. Instead, Schlegel, according to Huggler, "argues quite convincingly for a more important distinction between republicanism and despotism".

In the article "Representing the Vortex: Delacroix's Critique of Poe's Sublime", Andrew Kent-Marvick and Louis Marvick explore the figure of the vortex in the short story 'A Descent into the Maelström' by Edgar Allen Poe and the French painter Eugène Delacroix's critical reception of it. The inherent differences in the two media of literature and painting form the basis of a discussion of their ability for conveying the sublime.

In her article "Re-enchanting Art in Theory and Practice: Symbolism in Greece and Frixos Aristeus", Victoria Ferentinou analyses the oeuvre of Frixos Aristeus (1879–1951) as an example of re-enchantment in Greek symbolist art. Thereby she adds an important chapter to the scholarly exploration of symbolism and esotericism where the latter constitutes a cultural code which has to be taken into account in order to understand the symbolist works of art. What seems cryptic on the surface turns out to be esoteric imagery.

Tim van Gerven describes his newly finished PhD-project, *Scandinavism. Overlapping and Competing Identities in the Nordic World, 1770–1919*, in the article "Scandinavism: Wiring Nationalism in the North". In his dissertation, van Gerven seeks to re-evaluate the role of Scandinavism in the context of the more comprehensive European pan-nationalism. Rather than being a political failure – as it is often depicted – van Gerven argues that Scandinavism did have positive cultural implications. His conclusion is that pan-national movements such as Scandinavism constituted an underappreciated element in the development of Romantic nationalism.

Katrine Wonge Lohmann describes her ongoing PhD-project *Minerva Fiction as Nationalist Literature 1789–1830* in the article "The Local Gothic". Here, she examines the role of the Minerva Press in late eighteenth century as the settings of the Gothic novels moved from Southern Europe to Britain and thus became "local". The strategy of the publishing house was to establish aristocratic, Protestant heroes as Catholic enemies of the past served as a "proxy for contemporary Catholic enemies". Thereby, it is uncovered how literature was instrumentalized to political and national purposes.

Karen Klitgaard Povlsen reviews the biography on *Friederike Brun, Weltbürgerin in der Zeitenwende. Eine Biographie* by Kerstin Gräfin von Schwerin. According to Klitgaard Povlsen, this is a much-needed portrayal of a long forgotten, but nonetheless important historical German intellectual Friederike Brun, who spent most of her life in Denmark but published poems and travelogues in German. Despite minor criticisms, she calls it a well-researched and well-written biography, which contributes to the renewed interest in this remarkable woman.

Welcome to the new issue of *Romantik*.

Gísli Magnússon, on behalf of the editorial board

Articles

Peter Svare Valeur
(The University of Bergen)

'What is This Strange Language?' Reflections on
The Barbaric in Jean-Jacques Rousseau and
François-René De Chateaubriand

> There is not a book here, not a man to lend ear to me,
> to know what my words mean.
> All places are filled with barbarism and cries of wild animals,
> all are filled with the fear of hostile sound. (Ovid, *Tristia* 5, 12: 53–56)

Abstract
Examining the ideas of the barbarian and barbarism, this article considers and compares the work of Jean-Jacques Rousseau and François-René de Chateaubriand in both historical and poetical terms. I argue that both Rousseau and Chateaubriand present and identify with the figure of the barbarian as a means to make poignant questions regarding Enlightenment optimism and rationalism, and that both exploit it as part of their media theory of writing. While Rousseau primarily highlights being an outsider and chastiser of modern society, Chateaubriand stands mournful before the scene of history, a witness to an increasing array of ruins. Their approaches illustrate two diverging views: an eighteenth-century politics highlighting the necessity of action and emancipation, and a romantic nostalgia aware of irredeemable historical discontinuity.

Keywords
Incomprehensibility, 'Barbaric primordial situation', Medium, 'Prosopopée de Fabricius', Antimodernism

It is sometimes said that romantic literature explores the disorderly, wild, and unknown. Not only did writers set their stories in new and exotic places, as we see in texts like Bernardin de Saint Pierre's *Paul et Virginie* (1788) or Chateaubriand's *Atala* (1801). They also started to experiment with a language emphasizing, as Michel Foucault has put it, 'l'être sauvage et impérieux des mots' [the savage and unruly being of words].[1] Just as the places became more exotic, so the words and the structure of the literary composition became ever more unusual and experimental. Verbal landscapes were created which gave the im-

---
1 Michel Foucault, *Les mots et les choses* (Paris: Gallimard, 1966), 313. My own translation. Unless otherwise stated, all translations are my own.

pression of poets 'battling with language' and disrupting the fluidity of the written medium in order to heighten the expressive effects.[2] Unsurprisingly, the authors also became increasingly fascinated by the barbarian and the barbaric, etymologically pointing to language that is incomprehensible.[3] 'La poésie veut quelque chose d'énorme, de barbare et de sauvage' [Poetry must have something in it that is barbaric, vast and wild], Denis Diderot wrote in 'De la poésie dramatique' in 1761, linking poetry with the barbaric, unregulated, and sublime.[4] Not only did the barbaric involve verbal expression, however, but it also raised questions about individuality and authenticity: to a world steeped in conventions and burdened with what Freud would later call 'das Unbehagen in der Kultur' [the uneasiness in civilization], the barbarian appeared the only one in possession of natural and genuine feelings. From Rousseau's *bon sauvage* to Schiller's concept of the naïve, the late eighteenth-century toyed with the thought that barbaric impulses and forces would have a beneficial effect on society and culture at large. Few years before the 1789 revolution and the ensuing Terror, Diderot had seen the barbaric as a necessary ingredient in the regeneration of societies: 'une nation ne se régénère que dans un bain de sang' [A nation does not regenerate itself except through a bloodbath].[5]

This article sets out to document two stages in the era's attraction to the barbaric, one coming before and the other after the 1789 revolution. I begin with Jean-Jacques Rousseau, the self-proclaimed barbarian in the second part of the eighteenth-century, and end with François-René de Chateaubriand, the early nineteenth-century nostalgic whose *oeuvre* is astonishingly rich in barbaric imaginations. As will be shown, both these critics see the barbaric as a fruitful metaphor for thinking about history and historical developments, and their own role in it. Moreover, both wrote influential autobiographies where the barbaric is important to their literary *persona:* Identifying as barbarians, they draw attention to their own social status as outsiders and exiles. As we will see, crucial to this idea is also the poetics of defamiliarization, with the barbarian speaking and acting differently to others. Major differences in worldview separate the two, however, mostly in terms of their views on history. Rousseau, often seen as the first modern writer because he pioneered the cult of authenticity and genuine feelings, always presents himself as an outsider at odds with the civilized world. His vast autobiographical work demonstrates his pervading sense of confusion

---

2 In 1812, Adam Müller diagnosed, in the contemporary German context, the writers battling with language: 'ein Ringen mit der Sprache'. Adam Müller, *Zwölf Reden über die Beredsamkeit und deren Verfall in Deutschland* (Frankfurt am Main: Insel, 1967), 41.
3 In Greek, the word 'barbaros' means someone who does not speak Greek and does not follow classical Greek customs.
4 Denis Diderot, *Oeuvres esthétiques* (Paris Gallimard, 1997), 261.
5 Denis Diderot, *Oeuvres politiques* (Paris: Laffont, 1995), 635.

and alienation as a Swiss foreigner in the cultured Parisian society, and he repeatedly insists that he speaks the language of nature, a *barbarian* language, which Parisians have become too 'refined' to understand. His attitude in this regard reflects what Reinhart Koselleck has termed Rousseau's discovery of the 'aporia of progress', namely that the process of 'enlightening' and the striving for civilizational perfection inexorably lead to inequality, decline of morals, and loss of man's natural innocence. 'Progress produces decadence'.[6] Given his damning diagnosis, Rousseau deems the barbaric a necessary exit route to the reclaiming of individual freedom, and he makes it a governing principle of his own work.

While Rousseau exploits the barbaric in terms of his complex view on historical progress, Chateaubriand, who, according to Pierre Michel was throughout his life 'obsessed by the barbarians', connects barbarity to his poetics of death and doom, his embracement of *vanitas* and lost causes.[7] Claiming that 'life is a successive death', the barbaric, meaning the destructive, is for Chateaubriand the driving force of history.[8] More precisely, the modern era, which Chateaubriand dismissively coined 'la modernité', is infested by barbaric disfigurement: it has grown decadent and vulgar, with moral and aesthetic standards mercilessly sacrificed.[9] Thus, while Rousseau's barbaric imaginations reflect an eighteenth-century politics based on the belief in the individual's capacity for emancipation, Chateaubriand presents early nineteenth-century nostalgia and what Antoine Compagnon has called 'antimodernism', meaning a worldview where skepticism of progress and hatred of democracy conjoin with a rehashing of Christian dogma including hereditary sin.[10] Chateaubriand, who, due to his aristocratic background had to temporarily leave France during the Terror, felt that the revolution had created a tragic rupture between the old and the new, and that the new world lacked a clear point of orientation founded on respect for historical traditions and customs.[11] To him, the 'new' was synonymous with rudderless freedom and chaos exploited by opportunists, talentless upstarts, or blind fanatics. For Cha-

---

6 Reinhart Koselleck, '"Fortschritt" und "Niedergang"', in *Begriffsgeschichten* (F.a.M.: Suhrkamp 2006), 159–181, 177.
7 Pierre Michel, *Les barbares: 1789–1848. Un mythe romantique* (Paris: P.U.F., 1981), 83.
8 'La vie est une mort successive'. Chateaubriand, *Voyages en Italie* (Lausanne: Bibliothèque des Arts, 2003), 80.
9 On the cultural and historical context of Chateaubriand's coining of the term 'modernité', and his linking it to 'vulgarité', see, among others, Peter Svare Valeur, *Romantic Figures of Old Age. Readings of Chateaubriand, Eichendorff andn Wordsworth,* diss. (Oslo: University of Oslo Press 2012), 65–82.
10 Antoine Compagnon, *Les antimodernes, de Joseph de Maistre à Roland Barthes* (Paris: Gallimard, 2016).
11 This acute sense of historic discontinuity makes Chateaubriand more aware of the historical process than many of his contemporaries. See for instance François Hartog *Régimes d'historicité* (Paris: Seuil 2003), 85.

teaubriand unlike Rousseau, barbarism was not to heroically oppose the rules of the world and the establishment; rather, barbarism *is* the rule of a world grown anarchic and recalcitrant to true communal understanding. But Chateaubriand distinguishes between barbarians who know they are barbarians, and those who do not. A conscious barbarian is someone who knows that he is misunderstood or ignored, and that his words will meet deaf ears. As we will see, this is exactly how Chateaubriand goes about distinguishing himself in his writing: he glorifies himself as the martyr of incomprehension, as prophet of doom, and ['inutile Cassandre'[useless Cassandra].[12]

In this article, I will principally address barbarism in terms of these writers' autobiographic self-representations. Their concept of barbarism I see as primarily aesthetic and exhibitionist: They are artists and performers of barbarism, fashioning a heroic self-image of themselves as exiled, alienated, and misunderstood. The status as self-acclaimed barbarians enable them to present ideas and visions of the historical development at odds with Enlightenment optimism. Primarily, however, I will show that their aesthetics of barbarism conjoin with a media theory of writing. It is when confronted with the white page, the hardly legible epitaph, or a sentence from Bossuet quoted by a bird that the barbaric imaginations of these writers are at their most palpable and intense.[13]

---

12 With this term, Chateaubriand characterized himself after having held a speech on 7. August 1830 at the French Assembly where he forcefully criticized the in his view illegitimate new regime of Louis Philippe. *Mémoires d'outre-tombe,* vol.3, edition J.-C. Berchet (Paris: Livre de Poche 2007), 551.

13 There has been some texts on barbarism in Rousseau. Among the most recent, see Dieter Thomä, *Puer robustus. Eine Philosophie des Störenfrieds* (F.a.M.: Suhrkamp, 2016), 75–121. On the connection between Rousseau and Ovid, see Jean Starobinski, *La transparence et l'obstacle* (Paris: Gallimard, 2013), 137–159. On the concept of barbarism in French and notably German writers in the 18th century with some remarks on Rousseau, see Gérard Laudin, 'L'integration de la barbarie à la civilization: brutes, barbares, sauvages, despotes, et doctrinaires d'Iselin à Hölderlin', in *Le barbare. Images phobiques et réflexions sur l'altérité dans la culture européenne,* ed. Jen Schillinger and Philipp Alexandre (Bern: Peter Lang, 2008), 179–199. On barbarism in French writers after the revolution, including Chateaubriand, see the well-researched study by Pierre Michel, *Les barbares.* On barbarism in Chateaubriand, with particular emphasis on his historical essays, see Michel (ibid), Arlette Michel: 'Images des Barbares dans l'oeuvre de Chateaubriand', in *Bulletin de l'Association Guillaume Budé,* 1992, vol.2, 174–192, and some valuable remarks in Manfred Schneider, *Der Barbar. Endzeitstimmung und Kulturrecycling* (München: Hanser, 1997). Most of these studies tend to highlight philosophical or historical aspects, while they unfortunately downplay the barbaric as a means of autobiographical self-representation. – It should be noted that the crucial passages analyzed in my article have, to my knowledge, not previously been seen in the context of barbarism.

'Barbarus hic ego': Rousseau and the scene of writing

Fig. 1: Angélique Allais (née Briceau), *Portrait of Jean-Jacques Rousseau*, 1791, 24.5 x 21.5 cm, Bibliothèque de Genève.

A key episode in the life of Rousseau take place when, in the summer of 1749, he is on his way from Paris to Vincennes, hoping to see his then friend Denis Diderot. Under trees that, according to Rousseau, gave little shelter against the hot sun, and walking while reading a gazette, his eyes suddenly fall upon the advertisement of a writing contest with the following question: *Has progress of the arts and sciences strengthened or undermined the morals?* Rousseau comments: 'Si jamais quelque chose a ressemblé à une inspiration subite, c'est le mouvement qui se fit en moi à cette lecture; tout à coup je me sens l'esprit ébloui de mille lumières. (…) À l'instant de cette lecture je vis un autre univers, et je devins un autre homme" [If ever anything resembled a sudden inspiration, it is what that advertisement stimulated in me: all at once I felt my mind dazzled by a thousand lights. (...) At that moment I saw another universe, and I became a different person.]¹⁴

It is a scene of sudden insight, of momentous illumination, among others recalling – and this is certainly intended by Rousseau – the famous scene of conversion in Augustine's *Confessions* (8: 12, 29–30). In his autobiographical works, Rousseau dwells obsessively on this moment of epiphany. This was the moment, he tells, which sparked his career as a public intellectual, which formed the seed of what would later be his most prominent quality, namely that of a political writer who tells the truth about the flaws, injustices and mendacities that dominate the western societies. Highly agitated by what he had read, Rousseau states that he needed to sit down 'under an oak'. It is there that he starts to write down his response to the contest, calling it 'La prosopopée de Fabricius', a short text which would form the nucleus of his first major text, the prize winning essay *Discours sur les sciences et les arts* (1750).¹⁵

Rousseau, then, highlights the scene of writing; it was there, under that oak, that he 'became another man', and where his career as a writer of ardent, politically radical and sometimes scandalous texts, was inaugurated. *And:* it was there that Rousseau also became, at least in his autobiographical self-representations, a barbarian. How so? As a motto to *Discours sur les sciences et les arts* (as well as to his later *Dialogues: Rousseau juge de Jean-Jacques,* 1776), Rousseau chose a line from the Roman poet Ovid: *barbarus hic ego sum, qui non intelligor ulli* [Here it is I that am a barbarian, because the others do not understand me] (*Tristia* V, 10: 37). The line is from *Tristia*, the collection of poems Ovid wrote after having been banished from Rome and living in exile in Tomis, on the Black Sea. What Ovid refers to as 'the others', are the inhabitants of Tomis incapable of appreciating his Latin.¹⁶ Ovid's claim offers a perfect illustration of

---

14 Jean-Jacques Rousseau, *Confessions. Autres textes autobiographiques* (Paris: Gallimard, 1959), 1135, 351.
15 Rousseau uses a similar setting in *Essai sur l'origine des langues*, where he discusses the scene where language was invented, namely close to running water, where young people meet 'sous de vieux chênes'. Rousseau, *Essai sur l'origine des langues* (Paris: Gallimard, 2002), 106. Of course, the topos of sudden illuminations while sitting under trees goes back, at least, to Augustine's conversion under a fig tree.
16 In context, the Ovidian line is: *Barbarus hic ego sum quia non intelligor illis / Et rident stolidi verba Latina Getae* (V.10, l.37–38) [Here it is I that am a barbarian because the others do not understand me. Stupid as they are, the Getae laugh at my Latin.]. Ovid's *Tristia* tells of his experiences in Tomis, where he was forced to live after being expelled from Rome in 8 AD for unclear reasons. Ovid was 50 years old at the time. As we see, he complains about not being understood: 'the others do not understand me'. However, the second line – which symptomatically is not quoted by Rousseau – makes it clear that Ovid sees the Getae, the people living in Tomis, as the real barbarians, because they do not understand or appreciate his Latin. In this way, Ovid confirms the cultural hegemony of Rome.

Rousseau's moment of epiphany on the way to Vincennes. To see this, we must take a closer look at the short text which Rousseau managed to write down under that tree, 'La prosopopée de Fabricius'. The 'prosopopée de Fabricius' is, in fact, a powerful enactment of Ovid's statement, and stunning example of Rousseau's barbaric imagination.

It consists of Rousseau giving the word to Gaius Fabricius Luscinus, a Roman statesman of Republican era who is perhaps most known for having negotiated peace terms with Pyrrhus after the Roman defeat at Heraclea in 280 BC. Later Romans tended to praise Fabricius for his virtue and austere incorruptibility. In his text, Rousseau uses this historical figure to illustrate his main argument in his treatise, namely that the sciences and arts are in fact not beneficial, as usually held, but morally detrimental. Through his prosopopoeia, Fabricius rises from the grave, addressing Romans of a later period about how they have since been misled and corrupted. Here is the passage from *Discours sur les sciences et les arts:*

> Ô Fabricius! qu'eût pensé votre grand âme, si pour votre malheur rappelé à la vie, vous eussiez vu la face pompeuse de cette Rome sauvée par votre bras et que votre nom respectable avait plus illustrée que toutes ses conquêtes? 'Dieu! eussiez-vous dit, que sont devenus ces toits de chaume et ces foyers rustiques qu'habitaient jadis la modération et la vertu? Quelle splendeur funeste a succédé à la simplicité romaine? Quel est ce langage étranger? Quelle sont ces mœurs efféminées? Que signifient ces statues, ces tableaux, ces édifices? Insensés, qu'avez-vous fait? Vous les maîtres des nations, vous vous êtes rendus les esclaves des hommes frivoles que vous avez vaincus? Ce sont des rhéteurs qui vous gouvernent? C'est pour enrichir des architectes, des peintres, des statuaires, et des histrions, que vous avez arrosé de votre sang la Grèce et l'Asie? (…) Romains, hâtez-vous de renverser ces amphithéâtres; brisez ces marbres; brûlez ces tableaux; chassez ces esclaves qui vous subjuguent, et dont les funestes arts vous corrompent.

> [O Fabricius! What would your great soul have thought, if to your own misfortune you had been called back to life and had seen the pompous face of this Rome saved by your efforts and which your honourable name had distinguished more than all its conquests? 'Gods,' you would have said, 'what has happened to those thatched roofs and those rustic dwelling places where, back then, moderation and virtue lived? What fatal splendour has succeeded Roman simplicity? What is this strange language? What are these effeminate customs? What do these statues signify, these paintings, these buildings? You mad people, what have you done? You, masters of nations, have you turned yourself into the slaves of the frivolous men you conquered? Are you now governed by rhetoricians? Was it to enrich architects, painters, sculptors, and comic actors that you soaked Greece and Asia with your blood? (…) Romans, hurry up and tear down these amphitheatres, break up these marbles, burn these paintings, chase out these slaves who are subjugating you, whose fatal arts are corrupting you.][17]

---

17 Jean-Jacques Rousseau, *Du contrat social. Écrits politiques* (Paris: Gallimard, 1964), 14f.

With Fabricius as his mouthpiece, Rousseau paints a Roman civilization characterized by urban decadence, empty magnificence, love of arts, and moral decline. Claiming that the Romans are enslaved by those they had at first conquered, the passage addresses something Edward Gibbon in his *History of the Decline and Fall of the Roman Empire* (1776–1789) would explore in more depth, namely that Roman society was gradually undermined and destroyed because of its inability to politically and culturally integrate all its foreigners, or 'barbarians'.[18] However, although the text points to Rome, it should not be forgotten that Rousseau also has Paris in mind, and that the complaint and indignation which Fabricius vent before the 'splendeur funeste' is equally fitting when it comes to the estimation of the modern world. Jean Starobinski has noted that Rousseau 'wants to be seen as the true barbarian, the "peasant from Danube", who, having arrived in Paris speaks the language of nature, a language which the Parisians have unlearnt'.[19] Rousseau is thus on the one hand an outsider, but, taking the role and voice of Fabricius, he on the other invests himself with the authority to tell the Parisians the truth of their own moral decline. Although alienated and at the outside of the society he criticizes, Rousseau/Fabricius presents himself as the only one in possession of true knowledge of its moral and historical source.

Unsurprisingly, the historical authority Rousseau here flaunts builds on certain rhetorical tricks. For it is symptomatic that Rousseau/Fabricius fights with the same weapons he says have corrupted the Romans. Intriguingly, he blames the rhetoricians: 'Are you now governed by rhetoricians?' This is rather startling and not a little bold, given that Rousseau's passage is itself highly rhetorical. In particular, he makes use of the figures that Quintillian calls *indignatio* (Greek *deinôsis*) and *evidentia* (*enargeia*). The first consists in the speaker's ire, his indignation and 'strong exaggerations' faced with what is morally repulsive. Fabricius' words indicate what Starobinski has called Rousseau's 'extrémisme vertueux', his insistence on purity and simplicity as the sole compass of true morality. The other figure, *evidentia*, consists in presenting a clear visual impression of something, creating the illusion that it takes place before the speaker's very eyes. In the passage in question, the repetition of the deictic 'this/these' gives the impression that Fabricius positions himself immediately before this late Roman world: 'What is *this* strange language? What are *these* effeminate customs? What do *these* statues signify, *these* paintings, *these* buildings?' Clearly, confronted with this over- or perhaps pseudo-civilized world, Fabricius tends to appear as a barbarian, unable to understand his surroundings. But the effect of *evidentia* is to convince the hearers or readers that they share the same

---

18 On Gibbon and the barbarians, see J.G.A. Pocock's many-volumed work *Barbarism and Religion* (Cambridge: Cambridge University Press 1999f).
19 Jean Starobinski, *La transparence et l'obstacle* (Paris: Gallimard, 2013), 138.

position and moral perspective as the speaker. Like Fabricius, we, too, see and despair over this decadent world arising before us. It is a rhetorical manoeuvre to trick us into seeing the world with the eyes of its outsider and chastiser.

The 'prosopopée de Fabricius' encapsulates the historical tensions we found adumbrated by Koselleck: with a civilization seeking ever greater perfection primarily in aesthetics and science, the innocence of its inhabitants will inevitably be lost, and moral decline and alienation set in. For 'nos âmes se sont corrompues à mesure que nos sciences et nos arts se sont avancés à la perfection' [our souls have been ever more corrupted the more the arts and sciences have gained in perfection].[20] The 'aporia of progress' (Koselleck) – and this is Rousseau's point – leads ultimately to a fundamental clash, a cultural collision unleashing barbaric impulses. In the face of a society in thrall to scientific and aesthetic perfection, Fabricius calls for reckless iconoclastic *tabula rasa*-fantasies: 'brisez ces marbres; brûlez ces tableaux; chassez ces esclaves'! Rousseau's point seems to be that unbridled aesthetic and scientific progress will unleash destructive energies in the name of moral rejuvenation. In fact, Rousseau/Fabricius manifests not only a barbaric will to destruction, but also the urgency of extremism and fanaticism. Yet this is not something to be dismissive about; Rousseau wants to grasp the role of passion in politics, not as something negative, but as a source for change and potential emancipation. Indeed, approvals of a politics founded on strong passions and unbending wills – and which finds its source in religious enthusiasm – are frequently on show in *Discours sur les sciences et les arts*.[21] For instance, Rousseau refers to Omar, the caliph responsible for the destruction of the library in Alexandria:

> On dit que le calife Omar, consulté sur ce qu'il fallait faire de la bibliothèque d'Alexandria, répondit en ces termes: Si les livres de cette bibliothèque d'Alexandrie contiennent des choses opposés à l'Alcoran, ils sont mauvais et il faut les brûler. S'ils ne contiennent que la doctrine de l'Alcoran, brûlez-les encore: ils sont superflus.
>
> [They say that Caliph Omar, when consulted about what had to be done with the library of Alexandria, answered as follows: 'If the books of this library contain matters opposed to the Koran, they are bad and must be burned. If they contain only the doctrine of the Koran, burn them anyway, for they are superfluous.][22]

---

20 Ibid., 5.
21 Contrary to a host of eighteenth-century thinkers (including Voltaire) who tended to dismiss passion in politics, Rousseau hails what he calls the 'great passion' of 'civic fanaticism', seeing it as something that, at best, could unleash a politics of equality and emancipation. For a valuable discussion of Enlightenment views on fanaticism, see Alberto Toscano, *Fanaticism. On the Uses of an Idea* (London: Verso 2017), in particular, for the contrast between Voltaire and Rousseau 106–112.
22 Ibid., 28.

Again, we see Rousseau parroting the imperative of destruction. And again this imperative derives from an extremism of virtue, or political fanaticism.

Yet it is a crucial factor in this tableau of riotous energy and cultural clashes over historical developments that Rousseau situates these tensions within the medium of language. Indeed, this is where the barbaric impulses are most palpable. For Fabricius' question 'Quel est ce language étranger?' [What is this strange language?] creates an agonistic tension inside French itself, as if this very language is torn between elegance and barbarity, plagued by an internal difference which makes it impossible for Fabricius to understand it. On his way to Vincennes, Rousseau had felt the problems of language, or more precisely writing; during his moment of epiphany, it had been impossible to write down everything he had 'felt', he claims. 'Si j'avais jamais pu écrire le quart de ce que j'ai vu et senti sous cet arbre, avec quelle clarté j'aurais fait voir toutes les contradictions du système social, avec quelle force j'aurais exposé tous les abus de nos institutions (…)'. [If ever I could have written the quarter of what I saw and felt under that tree, with what clarity would I have revealed all the contradictions of the social system, with what force would I have exposed all the abuses of our institutions].[23] This is a language of insinuation, typical of Rousseau: all those injustices, contradictions and institutional flaws exist, but he was not able to write about them, as if there is a resistance within the medium of writing itself, setting up an obstacle between his ideas and their materialization. Rousseau uses *praeteritio*, writing about his failure to write. The spot on the road to Vincennes is thus not only the scene of inspiration, but also the scene of failure and *occasion manquée*. Perhaps that is why Rousseau then says that he only became a writer 'malgré moi': 'I became a writer almost despite myself'.[24]

This failure to connect the language of his mind with the language on paper is a frequent theme in Rousseau, and it points to a basic inner tension within language itself, a tension that raises the question of barbarism. In his autobiographical works, Rousseau often writes about his troubles regarding this medium. To take but one example:

> Mes manuscrits raturés, barbouillés, mêlés, indéchiffrables attestent la peine qu'ils m'ont coûtée. Il n'y en a pas un qu'il ne m'ait fallu transcrire quatre ou cinq fois avant de le donner à la presse. Je n'ai jamais pu rien faire la plume à la main vis-à-vis d'une table et de mon papier. C'est à la promenade au milieu des rochers et des bois, c'est la nuit dans mon lit et durant mes insomnies que j'écris dans mon cerveau, l'on peut juger avec quelle lenteur, surtout pour un homme absolument dépourvu de mémoire verbale, et qui de la vie n'a pu retenir six vers par cœur.[25]

---

23 Jean-Jacques Rousseau, *Confessions. Autres textes autobiographiques* (Paris: Gallimard, 1959), 1135f.
24 ibid., 1136.
25 Ibid., 114. See also, for a related passage, ibid., 351f.

[My manuscripts – crossed out, scribbled on, muddled, indecipherable – bear witness to what they have cost me. There is not one of them that I have not had to copy out four or five times before giving it to the printer. Seated at my table, with my pen in my hand and my paper in front of me, I have never been able to achieve anything. It is when I am out walking among the rocks and the woods, it is at night, sleepless in my bed, that I write in my head, and with what slowness may be imagined, especially since I am totally bereft of verbal memory and have never in my life managed to learn six lines of verse by heart.][26]

Rousseau suggests that writing is an alienating process, where the writer feels the estrangement of his own thoughts: the manuscript, being 'indéchiffrable', is a palimpsest whose content he is not fully able to understand. The 'hic' in Ovid's line *Barbarus hic ego* is thus, in the case of Rousseau, the paper itself, with its chaos of inscriptions and erasures: it is where the author is no longer able to understand his own mind.[27] 'La littérature, c'est la rature', Roland Barthes is reported to have said, and we can indeed see something of this in Rousseau's writings, so often skeptical of the whole business of writing. 'Raturer' means to overwrite, to erase, while the other adjective Rousseau uses: 'manuscrits *barbouillés*', etymologically suggests soiling and stains: impurity. Rousseau, re-writing his texts, seems constantly to be battling against the written 'barbouillage'. For the barbarian, the paper is scene of battle, of destruction, of erasure, and a search for purity.

No wonder, then, that Rousseau says he wants to flee the medium of writing altogether. His remarks epitomize what would later become a prominent topic of modernist writing: the horror of the paper. The point, however, is that this horror feeds into his wish for destruction, for just as Fabricius with his *tabula rasa*-fantasies rages against Roman artworks, so Rousseau rages against his own writing. There is a quest for purity and a battle against the sign that lies at the heart of Rousseau's writing, something that is indeed typical of 18th century writing altogether.[28] Rousseau presents this as his abhorrence of a putatively normative sphere of writing: 'Seated at my table, with my pen in my hand and my paper in front of me, I have never been able to achieve anything.' In a fragment from 'Mon portrait', he qualifies this further: 'Je ne fais jamais rien qu'à la promenade, la campagne est mon cabinet; l'aspect d'une table, du papier et des livres me donne de l'ennui, l'appareil du travail me décourage'. [I never do anything except when walking; the countryside is my study; seeing a table with paper and books bores me, the material used for writing discourages me][29] Rousseau can only

---

26 Rousseau, *Confessions*, translated by Angela Scholar (Oxford: OUP, 2008), 111.
27 A famous study of Rousseau's relationship to writing is Derrida, *Of Grammatology* 1997.
28 According to Juri M. Lotman, 'the striving for de-semiotization, the battle against the sign, is the basis of the culture of the Enlightenment'. Quoted in David Wellbery, *Lessing's Laocoon. Semiotics and aesthetics in the Age of Reason* (Cambridge: CUP, 2009), 35.
29 Rousseau, *Confessions. Autres textes autobiographiques*, 1128.

write by opposing the usual scene of writing, situating his writing in a sphere, the countryside, that of course does not facilitate it. This points to Rousseau's tendency, particularly in his old age, to write outdoors, what Claire Bustarret has called 'pratique d'écriture déambulatoire' [his ambulatory writing].[30] However, as we saw in his letter to Malesherbes, even this is difficult for Rousseau, given that on the road to Vincennes he was in fact incapable of writing down everything that was on his mind.

Barbarism, to Rousseau, thus involves awareness of a place, a 'hic', where language turns against itself, a place of internal opposition and *contra-diction*, accompanied by a dream of another place, a place ultimately free of language. The basic gesture of Rousseau is, as Starobinski has noted, to 'speak in order to escape the malediction of speech, to write about giving up writing'.[31] About his epiphany on the road to Vincennes, Rousseau had stated his wish to lay bare 'all the abuses of our institutions' and to show 'that man is naturally good and that it is through these institutions alone that men become bad.' The worst institution of society is, as Rousseau sees it, language. Ever again, Rousseau insists that language teaches men to become duplicitous and unnatural; the arbitrary nature of the signs gives them the opportunity to state falsehoods.[32] His self-proclaimed barbarism, which implies a fight against language, is thus also educative. For Rousseau, to educate men on the ills of society necessarily also involves demonstrating the ills of language.

A double perspective, highlighting both the aporia of progress and the barbaric regression to violence in the name of wounded morality but also individual freedom, makes out the drama of the 'prosopopée de Fabricius' and *Discours sur les sciences et les arts*. This clash is given a subtle expression by the frontispiece to the first edition. The engraving by the artist Jean-Baptiste Pierre shows Prometheus offering fire to man and to an ignorant satyr. This subject goes back (as Rousseau explains in *Lettre à M. Lecat*) to a story in Plutarch about a satyr

---

30 Claire Bustarret, 'La carte à jouer, support d'écriture au 18e siècle', in *Socio-anthropologie* (vol. 30, 2014), 83–98. An interesting example of this practice is the playing cards, the 'cartes à jouer', which Rousseau, apparently at the time he wrote *Rêveries du promeneur solitaire*, brought with him on his walks, and on which he wrote down short reflections and ideas; 27 of these cards are preserved, and many of these jottings contain erasures. The cards are reprinted, recto et verso, in the edition of *Rêveries du promeneur solitaire* by M. Eigeldinger, Geneva 1978.
31 Starobinski, *La transparence et l'obstacle*, 321.
32 An example of this is Rousseau's examination in *Lettre à d'Alembert* of the statement 'Je vous aime', which he sees as a trick used by libertines to fool women. And in *Émile*, Rousseau had warned against trying to feed the young pupil with too many words. The child is a little barbarian, and 'bon naturellement', and should not be misguided by the reign of words. See Schneider, *Der Barbar*, 160. In *Essai sur l'origine des langues*, he consequently celebrates the 'era of the barbarians' as a golden age when people did not write and hardly even spoke, each living on his own. Rousseau, *Essai sur l'origine des langues*, 93–96.

who, seeing Prometheus bringing fire and not knowing what it is, wants to caress and kiss the flame. Prometheus had shouted back at him: 'Satyr, you'll mourn your beard, for it takes fire when you touch the flame'.[33] Rousseau might have identified with the satyr, the barbarian, who has problems with handling the fire – or language. Yet he is also Prometheus, who has stolen the fire from the Olympian establishment and who with his book sets out to educate the reader. In the image of Prometheus and the satyr, the crucial overall ambition of the text such as it was exemplified in the 'prosopopée de Fabricius', namely to demonstrate the problems of the civilizational process, is clearly manifest. The flame of knowledge and the fire of barbaric impulse come together in a highly telling way. Prometheus offers to the barbarian the gift that is also a weapon of self-destruction – and the barbarian wants to kiss the language that at the same time destroys.

'New Place': Chateaubriand and the destruction of historical continuity

> Chateaubriand never looked for whatever is fruitful, traditional or eternal in the past or in death; the only thing that satisfied him was the past as past, and death as death. If required, he caused damage only to give himself all the more reason to cultivate his regret.[34]

In *Voyages en Italie*, a travel diary that together with his celebrated *Lettre à M. de Fontanes* records his experiences as a tourist in Italy in 1803, Chateaubriand frequently refers to barbarians. For instance, on 11th December 1803, he is in Tivoli outside Rome, studying some inscriptions on the graves. He concludes: 'Que peut-il y avoir de plus vain que tout ceci? Je lis sur une pierre les regrets qu'un vivant donnait à un mort; ce vivant est mort à son tour, et après deux mille ans je viens, moi, *barbare des Gaules,* parmi les ruines de Rome, étudier ces épitaphes'. [What could possibly prove more futile than this? I read upon a block of stone the expressions of regret that some living person bestowed on the dead; the survivor has perished in turn and I, *a barbarous Gaul,* arrive two thousand years later, and surrounded by the ruins of Rome pore over these epitaphs in their secluded retreat] (emphasis mine).[35] The utterance points to what might be termed Chateaubriand's poetics of epitaphs. Poring over the inscriptions of death, the author – a 'barbarous Gaul' – feels the futility of life and the insignificance of his own existence. Elsewhere he notes: 'La vie est une mort succes-

---

33 Rousseau, *Du contrat social. Écrits politiques*, 17.
34 Charles Maurras, quoted in Compagnon, *Les antimodernes,* 99. My translation.
35 Chateaubriand, *Voyages en Italie* (Lausanne: Bibliothèque des Arts, 2003), 56f.

sive' [Life is a successive death], and even more directly: 'Ma vie détruit ma vie' [My life destroys my life].[36] All existence is doomed from its outset, a malign process of self-disfigurement. This fatalist cult of auto-destruction is perhaps the most prominent feature of his autobiographical writing such as it materialized in his vast and characteristically titled *Mémoires d'outre-tombe* (1848–50), 'memories from beyond the grave'.

Chateaubriand's historical pessimism, which these remarks give witness of, offers the frame for his barbaric imaginations. Peter Fritzsche has lucidly zoomed in the historical background for the author's melancholy. 'In Chateaubriand's view, the revolution had shattered lines of social continuity, casting the present off from the past and thereby creating a "different race", exiles who had become estranged from their own time, that is, stranded in the present, and as a result came to read contemporary history as dispossession', Fritzsche points out.[37] A key word here is 'exile' and Chateaubriand's idea of himself as a cultural outcast in the aftermath of the 1789 revolution. In the following, I will give some examples of how this melancholy worldview creates the springboard for a poignant poetical *philology of barbarism*.[38] As we will see, Chateaubriand is the fatal archivist of barbarism, a merciless analyst of the leftovers of previous barbarian destruction. Unlike Rousseau, whose prosopopeia of Fabricius had a certain political and contemporary urgency, Chateaubriand views barbarism through the lenses of historical distance and with the acuity and vituperations of antimodernist nostalgia.[39] His sense of barbarism unfolds on the background of his poetics of inscriptions, as well as his ideas about posthumous survival.

A first example of this is a passage from his *Essai sur la littérature anglaise* (1836). This passage will tell us something about how Chateaubriand takes the Ovidian 'barbarus hic ego' in a completely different direction than Rousseau. The *Essai sur la littérature anglaise* itself is a long and well informed history of English literature from the Middle Ages to the present, also including Chateaubriand's translation into prose of Milton's *Paradise Lost*. Yet what is striking about the text is its pessimistic and even fatalistic conclusions. Sharing the conservative opinions of Edmund Burke who in *Reflections on the Revolution in France* had vehemently criticized the French revolutionaries for their *tabula rasa*-fantasies and hatred for inherited customs and institutions, and transporting Burke's pol-

---

36 Ibid., 80. And Chateaubriand, *Mémoires d'outre-tombe*, 2 volumes (Paris: Gallimard 1964), 585.
37 Fritzsche, *Stranded in the Present. Modern Time and the Melancholy of History* (Harvard: Harvard University Press, 2004), 55f.
38 Chateaubriand, *Essai sur la littérature anglaise*, ed. Sébastien Baudoin (Paris: Société des Textes Français Modernes, 2012), 95.
39 Compagnon finds that a rhetoric of vituperation is typical of anti-modern thinkers like Chateaubriand or de Maistre. See *Les antimodernes*, 169–181.

itics into a literary and aesthetic context, Chateaubriand diagnoses a modern anarchy of taste where inherited standards and canons, the 'renommées universelles', have been lost.[40] There is moreover little reason to have any hope for the future: 'Il est à craindre que les talents supérieurs n'aient à l'avenir pour faire entendre leurs harmonies qu'un instrument discord ou fêlé'. [It is to be feared that the most talented writers in the future will only have a flawed instrument on which to play their harmonies].[41]

This diagnosis finds its most stunning illustration in the following passage, perfectly encapsulating Roland Barthes' claim that Chateaubriand had a predilection for 'linguistic Apocalypse'.[42] Here, Chateaubriand considers the death of languages:

> Des peuplades de l'Orénoque n'existent plus; il n'est resté de leur dialecte qu'une douzaine de mots prononcés dans la cime des arbres par des perroquets redevenus libres; la grive d'Agrippine qui gazouilloit des mots grecs sur les balustrades des palais de Rome. Tel sera tôt ou tard le sort de nos jargons modernes: quelque sansonnet de *New-Place* sifflera sur un pommier des vers de Shakespeare, inintelligibles au passant; quelque corbeau envolé de la cage du dernier curé franco-gaulois dira, du haut de la tour en ruine d'une cathédrale abandonnée, à des peuples étrangers, nos successeurs: "Agréez les accents d'une voix qui vous fut connue; vous mettrez fin à tous ces discours." Soyez donc Shakespeare ou Bossuet, pour qu'en dernier résultat votre chef-d'œuvre survive dans la mémoire d'un oiseau, à votre langage et à votre souvenir chez les hommes.
>
> [There are Orinoco tribes that no longer exist; all that remains of their dialect is a dozen words uttered in the treetops by a few parrots enjoying their new-found freedom; Agrippina's thrush warbling Greek words from the balustrades of the Roman palaces. Such will be, sooner or later, the fate of our modern jargons: some starling will whistle verses by Shakespeare from an appletree at *New-Place*, incomprehensible to those passing by; having flown out of its cage, some raven belonging to the last Franco-Gallic priest will address foreign peoples, our successors, from the heights of a ruined tower of an evacuated cathedral: 'Accept these last accents of a voice that you once knew well. You put all my orations to an end'.
>
> Be Shakespeare or Bossuet, then, so that in the final outcome your masterpiece shall outlive your language and man's remembrance of you in the memory of a bird.][43]

The passage offers a series of laconically stated anecdotal oddities: First we are in America among Indians, then in Rome with emperor Claudius's wife Agrippina who according to Pliny the Elder owned a thrush fluent in the human language.

---

40 ibid., 495.
41 Chateaubriand, *Essai sur la littérature anglaise*, 489f.
42 Roland Barthes, *The Preparation of the Novel*, transl. by Kate Briggs (New York: Columbia University Press, 2011), 290.
43 Ibid., 493f. Chateaubriand obviously liked this passage so well that he included it, with some minor changes, in *Mémoires d'outre-tombe*.

Then we are at a place called 'New-Place' associated with Shakespeare, and finally we meet a raven quoting from Bossuet's famous funeral speech to the Prince of Condé (1687). The bravura of the passage is evident, yet also its pessimism. Our own French language will die out, Chateaubriand states. The conclusion is rather startling: the reader is exhorted to become a great writer, like Shakespeare or Bossuet, just in order to be remembered – not by man – but by a quoting bird.

There are a number of features in this text but the most telling in our context is its manifestation of what might be termed the *barbaric primordial situation*. When writing about the future death of French, Chateaubriand tacitly presupposes that his own work will eventually be just as incomprehensible and foreign as those of Shakespeare or Bossuet. Ovid's phrase about 'Barbarus hic ego' is thus transported into the future: 'you might understand me now, but not later'. The text is thus not only *about* apocalypse, but itself a prospective victim of it. Evidently, the downfall of common understanding and semantic chaos – the barbaric primordial situation – fascinated Chateaubriand, for whom the incommunicable, the ruinous and defective were the principal forces and dimensions of history.[44] Here, we see it in the example of the starling quoting Shakespeare, where the name for starling in French: 'sansonnet' contains both 'sans' and 'sonnet', so that the near-at-hand suggestion is that the 'sansonnet' quotes the sonnets of Shakespeare, but deprived of artful form. Equally, in the image of the raven quoting Bossuet, the suggestion is that the understanding of the speech is gone. Not for nothing, Bossuet is quoted as saying: 'Accept these last accents of a voice that you *once* knew well'. *Once,* but not anymore. In the apocalyptic landscape depicted by Chateaubriand, only birds remember the eloquence of Bossuet, the perhaps greatest orator of French Classicism.[45] Language, spoken by parrots having escaped from the cages of a civilization gone to pieces, has lost its human origin. Chateaubriand thus reverses the tradition among (Enlightenment) philosophers for seeing language as the mark of humanity and what sets man above animals. Bossuet's words have become what Rousseau termed 'ce langage étranger',

---

44 Denis Hollier has argued that Chateaubriand had a 'passion for utterances that have outlived their destination, that have survived the necessity and even the possibility of meaning, a passion for languages that a contextual mutation has released from the necessity of meaning anything at all, languages that exist without having to make[s] themselves heard'. See Hollier 1989, 'French Customs, Literary Borders', in *October* (vol. 49, 1989), 40–52, 50.

45 The specific authority and dignity of Bossuet's style has often been highlighted. According to the fine words of Paul Valéry, in his short sketch 'Sur Bossuet', the French bishop was the master of a rhetorical style centring less on thoughts than on architectonic form. Paul Valéry, *Oeuvres 1* (Paris: Gallimard, 1957), 499. This view was also held by Chateaubriand. In *Génie du Christianisme* (1802), he remarks that Bossuet spoke on behalf of 'le siècle de Louis', and that his orations represented the canonical expression of that great era. Chateaubriand, *Essai sur les révolutions. Génie du christianisme* (Paris: Gallimard, 1978), 866.

even if the context is different. These words are incomprehensible to those who hear them, those Chateaubriand calls 'foreign peoples, our successors'.

In contra-distinction to the Enlightenment myth of progress, Chateaubriand thus presents history as a process towards increasing precariousness, destruction and disorientation. Nothing less than the downfall of Christian civilization is manifested, with the cathedral in ruins, and no one capable of understanding, let alone appreciating, the artworks of the past. Chateaubriand has in mind a landscape of Babelian confusion (suggested by the image of the "ruined tower"), of exile and *psittacism*.[46] It is fitting that he has chosen Bossuet's last funeral speech, the one devoted to the prince of Condé. There, Bossuet had ended with stating that this speech would be his last ('You put all my orations to an end').[47] In his own passage, Chateaubriand exploits the pathos of the 'last word', using Bossuet in order to proclaim the funeral speech to the French language.[48] It will only live on in the memory of birds.

Is there nothing in the passage that opposes the bleak historical prophecy? Is Chateaubriand exclusively the fatalistic prophet of cultural apocalypse? Here we must turn to what is perhaps the passage's most crucial feature, its reference to 'New-Place' (written in English and in italics in the original). What is 'new' about this place? In fact, 'New-Place' was the name of Shakespeare's house in Stratford-upon-Avon where he spent his last years. However, in 1765, the then owner, a priest named Francis Gastrell, simply demolished both house and garden.[49] Thus, what once was 'new' had not only grown old but eradicated. Is not the fate of this house analogous with the state of literature in the modern age, Chateaubriand asks? The passage suggests that the future of literature will be one of homelessness where great literature will appear only as incomprehensible birdsong in a place whose link to the past is demolished.[50] Modern bar-

---

46 The word *psittacism* (after Latin *psittacus*, parrot) was coined by Leibniz, meaning a speech that is repetitive and mechanic. (The background for this neologism was Spinoza's ridicule, in *Tractatus theologico-politicus*, of people who say 'verba psittaci vel automati, quae sine mente et sensu loquuntur.' (13, 155/156) – 419: Spinoza had in mind people who uttered religious phrases not knowing what they meant).
47 'Agréez ces derniers efforts d'une voix qui vous fut connue: vous mettrez fin à tous ces discours'. Jacques-Bénigne Bossuet, *Oeuvres* (Paris: Gallimard, 1961), 217f. Note that Chateaubriand writes 'accents' instead of Bossuet's 'efforts'. In his discussion of Bossuet's text in *Réflexions sur les éloges académiques* (1821), Jean le Rond d'Alembert had played on the difference between 'efforts' and 'accens', something which may have inspired Chateaubriand. See d'Alembert, *Ouevres completes*, vol. 2 (London: Belin, 1821), 267.
48 See René Pommier, 'Le vieux corbeau et l'aigle de Meaux', in *La pensée du paradoxe*, eds. F. Bercegol and D. Philippot (Paris: PUP, 2006), 435–442.
49 On Gastrell and 'New-Place', see Ian Ousby, *The Englishman's England. Taste, Travel, and the Rise of Tourism* (London: Pimlico, 2002), 31f.
50 Chateaubriand was not alone in surmising that Shakespeare would not be understood in the future. Already at the beginning of the great Shakespeare-cult in Germany in the late 18th

barians like Gastrell will have destroyed the continuity between the past and the future.

However, this is perhaps not the whole picture, and there are signs that Chateaubriand was, at least partially, capable of unearthing something positive from what he viewed as the barbaric unfolding of history. This consists in his vision of the liberation of birds, his ornithological messianism. These birds, singing incomprehensibly from a 'pommier' [appletree] at 'New-Place', represents not only the downfall of human history, knowledge and tradition, of art and languages. Having escaped prior captivity, they also expose a 'new-found freedom'. Their new place is a place of freedom, where they live in post-apocalyptic bliss. Chateaubriand here proves himself a pioneer of romantic ecology, albeit an ecology that excludes and dismisses the continuing existence of Western civilized man as we know him. A poetics of survival in the wake of catastrophe surface in Chateaubriand's passage. While Ovid's place of barbarism was Tomis, and Rousseau's was Paris, Chateaubriand's 'New-Place' is the messianic ornithological future.

With his vision of the ruins of 'New-Place' as accommodation for the emancipated starlings of the future, Chateaubriand offers a succinct illustration of the historical *dynamics* of barbarism. This consists in how after destruction follows a complicated post-apocalyptic aftermath. In his *Lettre à M. de Fontanes*, Chateaubriand offers an illustration of this dynamics. As a tourist at the site of Villa Adriana, he reflects on the destruction of the house of the emperor Hadrian:

> Je rappelais les événements qui avaient renversé cette *villa* superbe; je la voyais dépouillée de ses plus beaux ornements par le successeur d'Adrian, je voyais les Barbares y passer comme un tourbillon, s'y cantonner quelquefois, et pour se défendre dans ses mêmes monuments qu'ils avaient à moitié détruits, couronner l'ordre grec et toscan du créneau gothique (...).
>
> [I thought of the events that had destroyed this superb *villa*; I saw it despoiled of its most beautiful ornaments by Hadrian's successor; I saw the barbarians passing by like a whirlwind, sometimes staying here; and, in order to defend themselves among these monuments which they had half destroyed, crowning the Greek and Tuscan orders with Gothic battlements.][51]

Hadrian's villa functions in the same way as Shakespeare's 'New-Place'. It offers habitation for past or future barbarians, be they Goths or birds. Chateaubriand, who as we remember had called himself 'a barbarous Gaul', sees himself as also

---

century, Herder had claimed in his highly influential essay on 'Shakespear' from 1773 that 'Shakspear immer mehr veralte!' (sic). Herder claimed that his own generation would be the last one capable of understanding his plays. Johann Gottfried Herder, *Schriften zur Ästhetik und Literatur* (F.a.M.: dkv, 1993), 520.

51 Ibid., 173.

part of this law of history. With his own philological archeology, he is himself a temporary pensioner in the villa devoted to the leftovers of catastrophe.

In a passage from his *Mémoires d'outre tombe,* we get a clear sense of the way Chateaubriand sees his work and its fate. He speaks about his excavations in 1829 at Torre Vergata, just outside Rome, near the tomb of Nero:

> J'irai ce matin a ma fouille: hier nous avons trouvé le squelette d'un soldat goth et le bras d'une statue de femme. C'était rencontrer le destructeur avec la ruine qu'il avait faite; nous avons une grande espérance de retrouver ce matin la statue! Si les débris d'architecture que je découvre en valent la peine, je ne les renverserai pas pour vendre les briques comme on fait ordinairement; je les laisserai debout, et ils porteront mon nom: ils sont du temps de Domitien.
>
> [I shall go to my excavation this morning: yesterday we discovered the skeleton of a Gothic soldier and the arm of a female statue. It was as though one had come upon the destroyer together with the ruin he had made; we have great hopes of finding the statue this morning. If the architectural remains which I am uncovering are worth the trouble, I shall not break them up to sell the bricks, as is usually done: I shall leave them standing, and they will bear my name. They belong to the time of Domitian.][52]

Chateaubriand contemplates the statue and its destroyer, the 'Gothic soldier' who is himself dead. History is thus, as he puts it, continual destruction, 'ruins of ruins', yet these ruins will also, given Chateaubriand's unearthing of them, enjoy posthumous fame.[53] It is within this thematic context of destroyed artworks, dead barbarians and posthumous survival that Chateaubriand posits his own work. He pursues a poetic and philological archeology which gives witness to the inherently barbarian tendency of history with its continuously destructive energies, and he presents his own name as one extra addition to this work of history; his name will figure on the 'bricks'. With the title of his autobiography in mind, we could say that he is speaking 'outre-tombe', from beyond his own grave.

Conclusion

As we have seen, both Rousseau and Chateaubriand use the idea of barbarism as a fruitful metaphor for historical contextualization as well as for autobiographical self-representation. Both deploy the notion of barbarism to make critical questions of the project of Enlightenment optimism and rationalism, and both exploit it in terms of their own poetics and reflections about the medium of writing. Diderot's claim that modern literature needs to manifest something 'barbaric, vast and wild' rings true for both of them. Be it through Rousseau's battle against

---

52 Chateaubriand, *Mémoires d'outre-tombe*, vol. 3, ed. Berchet, (Paris: Poche 2002), 334.
53 Chateaubriand, *Voyages en Italie*, 174.

the sign, or Chateaubriand's poetics of epitaphs, they both demonstrate a modern sense of writing, i. e. the experience with 'the savage and unruly being of words', which Michel Foucault saw as key to the modern idea of literature (or 'écriture').

In historical-philosophical terms, however, there are major differences between them. Rousseau, building on his diagnosis of the aporia of progress and of civilization, saw the urge to violence and barbarism as ultimately inevitable and even positive for individual freedom. Barbarism becomes a signal for a politics embracing the possibility of emancipation. His prosopopeia of Fabricius had started with a subjunctive: 'O Fabricius! What would your great soul have thought, if to your own misfortune you had been called back to life'. George Steiner has said about grammatical forms such as subjunctives, optatives and counter-factual modes that because they allow us to alter the world, they offer 'a nucleus of potentiality' and are as such 'the passwords of hope'.[54] For Rousseau, the idea of barbarism is a means to imagine something else and perhaps *better* than the current situation. This contrasts with Chateaubriand, whose bleak evocations of a cultural apocalypse present a fatalist (with the words of Maurras) cult of 'the past as past, and death as death'. Chateaubriand's depiction of the barbaric ur-situation, i. e. mutual incomprehension, thoroughly informs his portrayals of the ruins of historical discontinuity. However, as we saw, there remains glimpses of hope, not least in his reference to 'New-Place' with the starling singing from an apple tree. It perhaps merits attention that Shakespeare allegedly had planted not an apple tree, but a mulberry tree in his garden. The apple tree thus only exists in and through this *new* place planted in Chateaubriand's own text. His 'New-Place' thus underscores not only his creativity in subtly manipulating the tradition. Chateaubriand's 'New-Place' is itself something positive to come out of the prior barbaric destruction.

---

54 George Steiner, *Grammars of Creation* (London: faber and faber, 2002), 5.

Adrian Mioc
(University of Western Ontario, Canada)

Romantic Theories of Life: Coleridge and Shelley

Abstract
This article stages a dialogue between two texts that deal with the same subject matter. Coleridge's *The Theory of Life* and Shelley's fragment *On Life* are both attempts to define life or existence. The analysis will be organized in the following way: the first two parts will address the two theories separately, while the latter will put them side by side in a point by point comparison. This investigation aims to reveal important insights with respect to the worldview of each of the poets discussed which can subsequently be used in scrutinizing their poetical work as well. Overall, this article hopes to affirm its rather distinct relevance in the way it theoretically frames the meeting of two major personalities of the romantic Age.

Keywords
Life, Imagination, Philosophy, Poetry, Perception

Coleridge's *The Theory of Life* and Shelley's fragment *On Life* share a common topic without having influenced each other directly. Dated 1818, Coleridge's text was published in its final form only in 1848 as *Hints towards the Formation of a more Comprehensive Theory of Life,* while Shelley's writing was penned sometime in late 1819 but remained a fragment at the end of a notebook until it was published in 1932 together with two other short essays in *The Athenaeum.*

Both texts can be read as responses to the vitalist debate also known as the Abernethy-Lawrence dispute. The nature of vitality was indeed a hot topic in the period, and the discussion polarized many intellectuals from poets to scientists and surgeons. Both Percy Shelley and Coleridge had 'strong interests in the scientific developments of the day' and one could superficially disentangle the two theories of life in view of Coleridge's siding with Abernethy and Shelley's support of Lawrence.[1] In her book *Shelley and Vitality,* however, Sharon Ruston finds many overlapping ideas between Shelley and Coleridge. Generally

---
1 Catherine Packham, *Eighteenth-Century Vitalism; Bodies, Culture, Politics* (New York: Palgrave Macmillan, 2016), 209.

speaking, positions become blurry, as Lawrence himself did not fully argue for a mechanical or materialist position and thus never being truly engaged in a clearcut contradiction with Abernethy.[2] It has also been argued that despite his open rejection, Coleridge's theory has 'more in common with Lawrence than he cared to admit'.[3] According to Tilottama Rajan, Coleridge attempts to 'make friends' between John Hunter's ideas and idealist German philosophy.[4]

It is my understanding that the two texts have not been examined in a separate comparative analysis. Clayton Koelb's *The Revivifying Word* does mention them in his discussion on 'materialist spiritualism' and detects common features between the two poets as well. In this sense, Shelley's atheist beginnings cannot be considered 'absolute' while his late, *On Life* 'divorce from materialism was no more complete than his earlier marriage to it has been'.[5] Rather, the tendency towards unity, towards a 'necessary embodiment of spirit' remains common to both thinkers. This article springs from a need for fine-tuning and elucidation that aims to establish a valid benchmark that distinguishes between the two theories of life. From a theoretical high ground, the discussion finds both texts converging in the way they consider life in its most general aspect as being or existence. In this sense, one can mention Michel Henry stating that 'life is not a thing (as is the case of biological life, for example) but is precisely a knowledge (*savoir*), the first and foremost of all, that which all the others presuppose'.[6] When life turns out to be more than an ability to resist chemical decomposition or a biological affinity with vegetables and plants, the problematics of vitalism as a 'theory of the living body' is left behind.[7]

From a methodological point of view, Kant's philosophy will be called upon to act as a theoretical framework to mediate as a *tertium comparationis* [the third part of the comparison]. More obvious for Coleridge, the Kantian connection will be retraced, in Shelley's case, via Hume who is known to have triggered the awakening from the 'dogmatic slumber'.[8] Finally, since Coleridge's insights have

---

2 Sharon Ruston, *Shelley and Vitality* (New York: Palgrave Macmillan, 2005), 13.
3 Clayton Koelb, *The Revivifying Word. Literature, Philosophy, and the Theory of Life in Europe's Romantic Age* (New York: Camden House, 2008), 37.
4 Tilottama Rajan, *The Unavowable Community of Idealism: Coleridge and the Life Sciences*, in *European Romantic Review*, 14:4 (2003): 395–416.
5 Koelb, 46.
6 Michel Henry 'Ce que la science ne sait pas' in Ross Wilson, *Shelley and the Apprehension of Life* (Cambridge: Cambridge University Press, 2013), 35.
7 Ruston, *Shelley and Vitality*, 1. This is the reason why her book will provide fewer insights for this argument.
8 Wellek claims that 'there is no evidence for any real acquaintance of Shelley with Kant's philosophy' (182), but there is, at least, one letter to Thomas Hookham where Shelley says: 'I certainly wish to have all Kants [sic] works' in Frederick L. Jones, ed. *The Letters of Percy Bysshe Shelley*, vol. 1 (Oxford: Oxford University Press, 1964), 350. René Wellek, *Immanuel Kant in England 1793-1838* (Princeton: Princeton University Press, 1932).

Fig. 1: Gottlieb Doebler, Portrait of Emmanuel Kant, 1791, 28.5 x 33 cm. Ostpreußisches Landesmuseum.

already raised theoretical concerns, this inquiry will merely examine how the two texts connect without passing judgments about their validity.[9] Since the stake of this article is to highlight substantive differences between the two poets and to frame them theoretically, the analysis will not be confined to the two texts alone but will ramify to others as well.

1. Shelley's 'On Life'

Romanticism is known for its philosophical propensity and, generically speaking, the encounter between the two poets occurs in a similar manner. Mary Shelley recalls her meeting with Coleridge: 'Seeing Coleridge last night reminded me *forcibly* of past times – his beautiful descriptions, metaphysical talk & subtle

---

9 Critics like René Wellek have already voiced concerns with respect to a 'fundamental weakness, incoherence and indistinctness' present in Coleridge's philosophical writings. See Wellek, *Kant*, 68.

distinctions reminded me of Shelley's conversations – such was the intercourse I on[c]e dayly [sic] enjoyed', (italics mine).¹⁰

In an era when Kantianism, German idealism, or English empiricism become almost unavoidable touchstones, poets try to live up and respond to such challenges as well. Shelley affirms that life occurs at the level of perception: 'life, and the world' is 'that which we are and feel'.¹¹ Existence and feeling are seen in their togetherness, and Shelley is siding with philosophers, who established *esse est percipi* [to be is to be perceived] as their main theoretical principle. Perception is the mind's capacity to be affected by impressions which are recorded as modifications of one's state of being. Impressions originate in either ideas or external objects and are perceived by what Shelley calls intellect or the 'one mind'. The intellectual perspective presents life as unity, but this 'one mind' is not identical with the subject or the 'I, the person who now write and think'.¹² The process of perception occurs prior to the formation of the transcendental subject that actively organizes representations according to forms of intuition and the requirements of the categories of understanding.¹³

The unity of the intellect grants the display of 'various subjects' or personas like '*I, you, they*' which endure as mere 'marks' that do not acknowledge an 'actual difference.' Modifications of the 'one mind,' these distinctions stay nominal as different or arbitrary names that still point to the same reality. Hence, changes remain on a formal level and do not manage to damage this unity. This perspective allows for dissipated or broken off parts to retain the ability to still be attributed to the same substance. While acknowledging plurality, this substance – a synonym with existence – does not undergo a dualism that would split it between two distinctly separated entities even when considering the two sources of impressions: the material underlying external objects or as the spiritual that frames ideas.¹⁴ Earl Wasserman's partially amended idea of a 'monistic idealism that identifies the One Mind with Existence' still captures the way in which the perceiving party is not qualitatively different or clearly distinguished from what it

---

10 Paula R. Feldman and Diana Scott-Kilvert, Eds. *The Journals of Mary Shelley 1814–1844*, vol. 2 (Oxford: Clarendon Press, 1987), 474.
11 Patrick Donovan and Cian Duffy. Eds. *On Life* in *Percy Shelley. Selected Poems and Prose*, (London: Penguin Classics. 2017), 540. Hereafter OL. The *Defence of Poetry* repeats the same idea: 'All things exist as they are perceived.' (Ibid. 576). Hereafter DP.
12 OL, 542. 'Let it not be supposed that this doctrine conducts to the monstrous presumption, that I, the person who now write and think, am that one mind. I am but a portion of it'.
13 Even though Kant's thinking subject remains undetermined, it still has the certainty of the Cartesian cogito.
14 Aristotle states that 'indeed the question that was, is and always will be asked – and always will cause difficulty – that is the question what being is (*to on*)'; a question which he also equates with "what is substance"'. W. D. Ross, trans. *Metaphysics*, Book VII, 1 1028b (Oxford: The Clarendon Press, 1924), 153.

perceives: 'His own mind is all things to him', says the poet in his *Speculations on Metaphysics*.[15]

The act of perception happens by itself 'with or without or (conscious n.n.) will' and turns out be unavoidable in the same way as one cannot shun life understood as 'that which includes all.' The 'certainty' Shelley mentions emerges from the *omnitudo realitatis* [the totality of all realities], but to just posit the identity of *esse* and *percipi* is a fairly general statement and needs further clarification. Bishop Berkeley is the first thinker that comes to mind, but his immaterialism does not fully cover Shelley's propensity towards sensation and empiricism in general.[16] Kant's philosophy, however, with its orientation towards sense experience will explain the bond in a way that will prove useful to both Shelley and Coleridge. For the 'sage of Koenigsberg', 'perception... is the sole mark of actuality'.[17] 'Actuality is at the same time a connection of it (i. e., a thing) with perception'.[18]

Manfred Frank says that Kant often uses *Wirklichkeit*, *Dasein* or *Existenz* as synonyms and states that 'the characteristic of being absolutely posited falls into the same group with that of the Being of sense impressions'.[19] The experience of sense perception is the only way the German philosopher can determine 'whether a concept has an existential (*daseienden*) content or whether we only think so'.[20] Perception is ontological as it records the impressions generated by a thing that exists; the thing can thus be confirmed as the cause of these impressions. Even if these raw or wild sense impressions are still subjective (i. e., the subjective side of perception) and cannot become an object of sensible intuition and thus used for knowledge, Kant cannot just dismiss or elude them. Because they must be thought as existing without being known, they pertain to the noumenal realm. In addition, the fact that they can only be thought makes them intelligible or perceivable by the intellect. As an aside, Kant's phenomenological approach will describe this realm as a marionette-like living ruled by necessity that cannot accommodate a cognizing subject that is able to claim her transcendental freedom.[21]

---

15 Harry Buxton Forman, ed. *The Prose Works of Percy Shelley* (London: Reeves and Turner, 1880), 293. Hereafter SM. See also Earl Wasserman, *Shelley: A Critical Reading* (Baltimore: Johns Hopkins University Press, 1971), 113. For an extended discussion that also refers to On Life see also Cian Duffy, *Shelley and the Revolutionary Sublime*, (Cambridge: Cambridge University Press, 2005), 65-73.
16 The idea is underscored by critics like Pulos or Duffy. See for ex. Cian Duffy, *Shelley and the Revolutionary Sublime*, 65.
17 Immanuel Kant and Norman Kemp Smith trans. *Critique of Pure Reason*, A225/B272-3 (New York: Modern Library, 1958), 243. Hereafter CPR.
18 Ibid. A235/B87 note, 252. Addition mine.
19 Manfred Frank and Elizabeth Millian-Zaibert trans. *Philosophical Foundations of Early German Romanticism* (Albany: SUNY Press, 2004), 63.
20 Ibid.
21 In a mysterious sub-chapter of his *Critique of Practical Reason* entitled 'Of the Wise Adap-

Shelley finds the very approach to life or existence to be permeated with ambiguity and contradiction. Even though life is an astonishing event, one still ends up being 'struck with admiration at its transient modifications'. This 'mist of familiarity obscures from us the wonder of our being' but this event can be both good and bad as it both 'critiques and fosters' life.[22] Ross Wilson is also right to emphasize that the mere act of 'living on' will lead to a loss of the 'apprehension of life'. While sensations inherently diminish in 'degrees of force' (Shelley) or 'vivacity' (Hume) as they become thoughts, habit and repetition will break the continuity.[23] However, since their difference is played out only as a difference of degrees (not one of kind), the lost apprehension can be restored even if it is felt as a break from the external world of nature. Abiding in a *plenum* [fullness] that contains everything, implies that the underlying unity or substance cannot be damaged. The human being becomes thus 'incapable of imagining to himself annihilation,' or, better said, the poietic ability of its imagination can create 'anew the universe, (even) after it has been annihilated in our minds.' The awareness or 'evidence,' and not the fullness as such, merely slips into a rather unconscious 'depository' from which the 'living spirit' present in words can still 'revivify' it.[24]

In contrast to perception or the uncontrollable (or accidental) flow of internal and external impressions, apprehension can be lost because it involves an act of synthesis, of distinguishing and gathering different impressions in a manifold in order to make empirical consciousness (*Wahrnehmung*) possible. When the synthesizing ability cannot keep up processing or being synchronous with the ongoing queue of impressions, the words that represent them lose their symbolic value and 'become, through time, signs for portions or classes of thoughts instead of pictures of integral thoughts'.[25] The loss of the *esse* of perception in apprehension signifies a disconnect from their generative origin that grants them a synthetic totality on a vertical or depth level. Hence, they end up abiding only on a temporal or horizontal level that is fitting for reason's analytic approach. From

---

tation of Man's Cognitive Faculties to His Practical Vocation', Kant explains what would happen to us if we were to gain access to the noumenal domain. Immanuel Kant and Thomas Kingsmill Abbot trans. *The Critique of Practical Reason* (New York: Dover Publications, 2004), 79. Shelley's idea of necessity is indebted to Hume, as we will see.

22 Ross Wilson, *Shelley and the Apprehension of Life* (Cambridge: Cambridge University Press, 2013), 19.

23 The affinity between them has been discussed, among others, by David Lee Clark. See Percy Bysshe Shelley and David Lee Clark ed. and introd. *Shelley's Prose. Or the Trumpet of a Prophecy* (Albuquerque: University of New Mexico Press, 1966), 182.

24 'We are ourselves the depositaries of the evidence of the subject which we consider'(SM). In 'To Constantia' the dissolution does not lead to a void but amounts to having a life in another person. 'I have no life, Constantia, now, but thee (...)'. For a detailed analysis of this aspect see Clayton Koelb's *The Revivifying Word: Literature, Philosophy, and the Theory of Life in Europe's Romantic Age* (Columbia: Boydell & Brewer, 2011).

25 DP, 562.

this point of view, thoughts turn out to be products or parts that are considered only separately as parts without being contemplated intellectually in their integrity or belonging to a whole.

Veiled by a 'mist of familiarity', the process of apprehension will become scripted. The 'habitual sense' and its 'repeated combinations' will merely order impressions mechanically or schematically. The same overarching rule is applied to all impressions which are now perceived as identical. They are no longer as merely similar while containing infinitesimal differences and nuances. The live feed of perceived sensations becomes clouded or obscured and imagination (not reason), with its more powerful capacity to synthesize will have to be called upon to fix the problem.[26] Proust offers a reminder that: 'the real voyage of discovery consists not in seeking new landscapes, but in having new eyes' which means 'defamiliarizing the familiar' in Ruston's words.[27]

Not by breaking through the illusory veil of transitory appearances that is now obstructing the process of apprehension is this achieved, though. Shelley propounds a 'philosophy of the future' that does not seek to repair its relation to the past. There is no need for that because the relation between things has remained a 'uniform' and 'constant conjunction of events.' Apprehension does not aim to catch up for lost impressions, but rather creates 'anew the universe' establishing its world in a 'happier form again'.[28] This is not a gesture of recovery from the ruins of a destructive event, as Bate argues: 'an attempt to recover the very thing which has been destroyed so that art can be made'.[29] Shelley's repetition will come close to a Deleuzian 'repetition into difference' that works based on a differential principle that creates new qualities. Such qualities abide beyond aiming to recuperate the very same relation to a previously apprehended event; the latter scenario would bring about a relative quality or a quality centered on a relation. New qualities are vitalizing or enlivening as they discover 'before unapprehended relations of things' while turning the mind into 'the receptacle of a thousand unapprehended combinations of thought'.[30]

---

26 Shelley believes that 'the human being...is not a moral, and an intellectual-but also, and pre-eminently, an imaginative being'. SM, 293. For Kant, the synthesis of the imagination or reproduction constitutes the second level after the synthesis of apprehension.
27 Ruston, 148.
28 I am referring to the line from *With a Guitar. To Jane:* 'died in sleep and felt no pain/ To live in happier form again'. Shelley, *Selected*, 504.
29 Jonathan Bate, *The Song of the Earth* (London: Picador, 2000), 78. Bate believes that the repetition brought about by the 'again' is redundant and excessive. Repairing an already broken relationship or link implies a substantial dualism and introduces mediation as a third term that will trigger a *regressus ad infinitum* [infinite regress]. A maintained unity of substance, however, allows for the knowledge of the tree to be transmitted and actualized immediately in the guitar.
30 DP, 565.

Put differently, imagination with its higher degree of consciousness or detachment from external things can 'defeat the curse which binds us to be subjected to the accident of surrounding impressions'.[31] It is thus able to create 'a being within our being' which allows the possibility of constructing a similar yet better (i.e., cosmos-like) universe that still corresponds to the real one. This expression or presentation can 'startle' the apprehension of life because it can make one feel 'again' the continuity between existence and perception. The most appropriate context for that is poetry because imagination is its primary tool. As an aside, one will now realize why every language was poetry in the beginning as well: even though words are created arbitrarily by the imagination, they can be arranged in a way in which they become able to express their poietic or generative origin and thus revive the substantial link with existence.

With respect to the disagreement between Bloom and Ruston concerning Shelley's rejection of 'natural perception,' one can add that imagination will overcome the level of perception whether the poet takes his inspiration from external/natural stimuli or not.[32] Overall, Shelley's poetry is still not as "idea-oriented" as Blake's which would decisively reject 'vegetative nature.' The important aspect is the restitution of the 'apprehension of life' (i.e., the relation between existence and perception) because it enables the possibility of the second step: the relation between perception and expression in a chain 'which at once connects, animates, and sustains the life of all.' This event is described as a recollection of 'our sensations as children' when 'we less habitually distinguished all that we saw and felt, from ourselves'.[33] Our perspective becomes unitary as everything 'seemed as it were to constitute one mass'. Those who have such child*like* poetic personalities 'feel as if their nature were dissolved into the surrounding universe, or as if the surrounding universe were absorbed into their being. They are conscious of no distinction. And these are states which precede, or accompany, or follow an unusually intense and vivid apprehension of life'.[34]

To illustrate the before-mentioned ambiguous aspect, one will say that not even rekindling the awareness of the "big picture" – the contemplation of the eternal beyond the transient – is enough to restore the apprehension of life.[35] Such a direct contemplation of the miracle of life cannot provide a definite answer either. The miraculousness of the miracle can only be expressed as a matter of

---

31 DP, 576.
32 See Sharon Ruston, *Shelley and Vitality* (London: Palgrave Macmillan, 2005), 185.
33 OL, 542. In the same sense, we become merely *like* children and don't jump back in time and become children again.
34 Ibid.
35 OL, 540: 'What are the revolutions of the globe which we inhabit, and the operations of the elements of which it is composed, compared with life? What is the universe of stars, and suns, of which this inhabited earth is one, and their motions, and their destiny, compared with life?'

degrees and will therefore be felt or perceived just subjectively. Our transcendental consciousness cannot find an objective measure or rule that could grasp and present it as an intuition that can be cognized. Hence, the very certainty of life turns out to be 'at once' 'so unfathomable.' This direct or immediate cognition, this intellectual intuition contains and becomes its own liability, but Shelley is not ready to simply discard it. He explains it positively as a safeguard put in place for our protection. Similar to what Walter Benjamin would later call a 'dialectical image', having to face something we cannot handle (the Gorgon face of Medusa or the sight of the naked Goddess Diana) will both impede and protect us from seeing life as it is. The 'mist ('veil' in Defence) of familiarity' can be deemed as a beneficial concealment as well, because it will 'shield' us from the sublimity/intensity of the miracle of life. Geoffrey Matthews suggests the same ambiguity when he says: 'a veil is now of ugliness concealing beauty, now of beauty concealing ugliness'.[36] Further to Ross Wilson's point regarding Shelley's resistance in 'rendering a definable *theory* of life', one will say that even when facing such ambiguity, one should not forfeit the possibility of theorizing altogether; thought and reason can still be used as 'instruments' of the imagination.[37] Neither steeped in a worthless illusion or error nor grasping, directly, the absolute mystery of existence, the condition of the human being seems suspended in the middle. From such a floating or unattached/absolute position, however, one is *free* to acquire a sense of rhythm, of harmony with the Heraclitan 'river of life' (Deleuze's 'pure process') that will enable an adequate expression.

Even as it marks the beginning of philosophy, this astonishment is a complex event that overawes the mind's capacity to grasp it. Shelley says that such an event will 'absorb and overawe the function of that which is its object'.[38] Since it includes all, life absorbs everything into itself while canceling the possibility of an external perspective from which the mind can turn it into an object of cognition and thus assign it a function. This finding is significant because if mind and body, thoughts and sensations are the two domains (i.e., attributes) that give us access to existence or nature, and the mind is prohibited from providing any knowledge about what life is, about how a thing is in its existence, it becomes clearer why Shelley is insisting that one will have to relate to life through the sensible side. Kant's rejection of metaphysics could also be mentioned in this context, but even a rationalist like Spinoza would agree with the approach. Finding an answer to the question 'what is life?' is far from over, though. As Shelley puts it, life and being is 'the line in which all things are contained' and will include all other forms of life

---

36 Geoffrey Matthews, 'A Volcano's Voice in Shelley' in *Shelley: Modern Judgments,* ed. R.B. Woodings (London: Macmillan, 1968), 164.
37 Wilson, 19.
38 OL, 540.

(i. e., biological life). However, it is also 'the point to which all things are referred,' the point which all our inquiries are directed towards.[39] Neither of the two can be reached, because life is, at once, both the 'the circumference and the center,' both the context or the framework and the goal or the concept.

Shelley will still not adhere to a radical skepticism that would leave a mere 'vacancy': the very revelation of life as an absolute or un-relatable mystery is not for nothing. It is true that 'it is vain to think that words can penetrate the mystery of our being!', because words can neither grasp the mystery of life as such or the absolutely posited (*an sich*) existence of a thing.[40] However, they will still expose our ignorance: 'Rightly used they (i. e., words) may make evident our ignorance to ourselves, and this is much'.[41] The 'education of error' rests on 'rightly' because one can still find 'adequate terms' to express the thing as an 'object of thought.' At this point, one can begin to understand the connection between perception and expression, between *Vorstellung* and *Darstellung*. In short, one can say that if life, in its general aspect, will remain an unreachable, yet enticing mystery, its particular aspect or the way a thing relates to the perceiver may still offer valuable insights.

Even if this approach does not bring about a 'new truth', any additional information about life (i. e., 'it gives us no additional insight into our hidden nature'), Shelley is convinced that this method can still yield valuable results.[42] To accomplish that, one needs to be reminded of two things: sensations constitute just the subjective side of intuition, and, as apprehension is lost and imagination gets involved, its synthesis will cut off the continuity or link to the real world. The latter aspect will constrain Shelley to conclude together with the 'philosopher' Shakespeare that 'the solid universe of external things' is 'such stuff as dreams are made of.' Even if this position is contrary to one's beliefs or convictions (i. e., 'our persuasions may struggle against it'), it must still be accepted as a truth based on the validity of its deduction.[43]

Setting out from perception or existence as opposed to positing reason or the mind first, is also significant because the latter 'cannot be the basis of all things, as the popular philosophy alleges'. Without having access to the knowledge of the origin of things, the mind 'cannot create' or express, ontologically speaking, 'a being within our being.' It will have to be merely included, just like everything else, as a passively perceptive product of existence, of that 'which includes all.' This statement does not discredit the mind because, even as a created instance, the mind is not useless: without being able to grasp how something came into being,

---

39 OL, 541.
40 Ibid.
41 Ibid.
42 Ibid.
43 Ibid.

its findings or knowledge will just have to be restricted to phenomena only. In other words, one cannot cognize how a thing exists in itself (*an sich*) but one can still *know* it phenomenally in the way it appears to us, in the way it presents itself in our perception. The idea is significant because the appearance we perceive can be considered a shadow of a substance which, even though it is 'less vivid than the substance,' even though it has been broken off, it can still be 'attributed' to the thing in nature because it contains its essence.[44] In other words, it retains or preserves the originary imprint. Shelley quotes Bacon saying that 'these similitudes…are finely said to the same footsteps of nature impressed upon the various subjects of the world'.[45] At this point, Shelley and Kant part ways.

Even though they agree that knowledge comes about through the mind's understanding, the poet is not concerned with securing a rule according to which this is supposed to take place. He is not interested in ensuring a condition of possibility prior to the cognitive event which implies determining the unity of a thinking subject that can hold the manifold of intuitions together. This consideration introduces the context of the transcendental apperception which requires a unity or synthesis that is different in kind from that of empirical consciousness. More importantly, Shelley will not rely on such a *stable* structure that will always inform or stamp his subjectivity in the same or identical way. We remember him authorizing 'modifications' of the subject which resonates with the Humean 'bundle of perceptions.' This means that he will just preserve this rather flexible unity that was already established by the intellectual perspective and his justification would be the following: if 'various subjects' are affected in similar ways by impressions, one can still presuppose a certain constancy or stability that constitutes itself as a network of relations or 'similitudes.' Even if 'all men' do not 'observe the same(/identical) order,' the similarity can still be considered a good enough ground to wait for knowledge or cognition without having to involve yet another organizing *a priori* instance to order impressions. Unlike Keats, Shelley does involve thought (i.e., conscious perception or apperception) and reason just not prior or transcendentally, but rather *after* imagination experiences sensations.[46] Thus, 'reason is to imagination as the instrument to the agent, as the body to the spirit, as the shadow to the substance'.[47]

The fact that a substance can be confirmed to generate a shadow not only maintains continuity but also validates the law of causality in the context of nature.

---

44 Spinoza's definition of the attribute points in the same direction: 'By attribute, I mean that which the intellect perceives as constituting the essence of substance.' Edwin Curley trans. *The Collected Works of Spinoza*, vol. I (Princeton: Princeton University Press, 1985), 25.
45 DP, 562.
46 Keats's relationship to thought can be further nuanced. I am referring here to his 1817 statements.
47 DP, 561.

This does not suggest, however, that causality *exists* in nature. For Shelley, 'cause is only a word expressing a certain state of the human mind with regard to the manner in which two thoughts are apprehended to be related to each other'.[48] Emphasizing the merely nominal value of causality will also underscore his positive variant of skepticism. Shelley agrees with Hume when he says: 'we know no more of cause and effect than a constant conjunction of events'.[49] One cannot gain knowledge of the first cause in the causal chain; such prerogative would grant the ability to actually generate the thing while placing the mind at 'the basis of all things' as well. Yet without unveiling the ultimate mystery, causality can still be considered a valid law of nature. On the one hand, causality is still only a 'state of the human mind' and not a heuristically or 'subjectively necessary' connection like in Kant; it does leave room for the question whether spring is far behind when winter is here. On the other hand, however, it is more than an regulative judgment that is based on 'the systematic unity of nature'.[50] In a scenario in which a shadow can be attributed backwards or retroactively to a substance in a way that would recover the apprehension of life, one can also put forward that causality is able to 'prophesize' an event in nature happening sooner or later. A distinction of degrees provides more determining power than a reflective judgement.

2. Coleridge's 'Theory of Life'

Shelley's intellectual perspective warrants his reservations with respect to 'materialism and the (dualistic) popular philosophy of mind and matter'.[51] Coleridge is no stranger to an anti-materialistic position either. For him, life can neither be confined to matter nor can it be projected outside it in an idealistic way. His solution aims to unify the two trends of thought which translate into overcoming the Cartesian dualism. Critics like Sharon Ruston have pointed to the fact that the two poets also share a propensity towards vitalism. In *Shelley and Vitality,* she corroborates that Shelley's imagination 'has been characterized as vital', but adds that 'S. T. Coleridge had similarly called the imagination "essentially vital" for this same reason'.[52] Shelley's concept of vitalism, however, is utterly devoid of 'any human interest.' Mary Shelley suggests this lack of anthropomorphism when speaking about *The Witch of Atlas* and Denise Gigante underscores the

---

48 OL, 542.
49 In his article 'Shelley, Godwin, Hume and the Doctrine of Necessity,' Frank B. Evans draws attention to this aspect even in *Queen Mab.* see *Studies in Philology* 37 (1940): 632–40.
50 CPR, A650-668/B678-696, 537.
51 OL, 542. Addition mine.
52 Ruston, 164.

idea by saying that 'those who suffer are about as substantial as a mist or a cloud'.[53]

The agreement between the two poets seems to run deeper still since the author of *Kubla Khan* also recognizes the value of perception and its relation to the perceiver: 'our reason convinces us that the quantities of things, taken abstractedly as quantity, exist only in the relations they bear to the percipient; in plainer words, they exist only in our minds, *ut quorum esse est percipi*'.[54] Owen Barfield points out that for Coleridge 'nature, so far as it has form and quality, is a compound of thoughts and perceptions'.[55] While sharing with Shelley an all-inclusive notion of life – 'what is not Life that really is' – it can be argued that Coleridge's notion of unity is different though. 'I define life as the principle of individuation, or the power which unites a given all into a whole that is presupposed by its parts'.[56] This unity conveys more distinction to the individual part that contains the whole it was generated by. The whole is organized by a centripetal force that keeps the parts together as a 'unity in multeity'.[57] It is also worth noting that in his third essay 'On the Principles of Sound Criticism', the same unity is defined as the principle of beauty which 'contemplated in its essentials, that is in kind and not in degree, is that in which the many parts, still seen *as many*, becomes one'.[58] Parts compose the whole as *disjecta membra* [scattered fragments] that acquire individuality by engaging in a relation to it. The four types of relationship mentioned by Coleridge have been discussed by Owen Barfield.[59]

The whole is no longer 'actual' but just 'presupposed'. It can only be only 'presupposed' because it cannot be 'accounted for:' 'to account for a thing is to see into the principle of its possibility, and from that principle to evolve its being'.[60] One cannot 'account for' a thing because one cannot state 'something prior to the thing accounted for, as the ground or cause for that thing.' The awareness of this shortcoming points to the irreconcilable split between what is experienced and what can be said about it. Forgoing to understand or conceptualize life by means of a sufficient cause – an idea shared by both Kant and Shelley – does not imply

---

53 Denise Gigante, *Life: Organic Form and Romanticism* (New Haven and London: Yale University Press, 2009), 166.
54 Samuel Taylor Coleridge and Thomas Ashe col. "*Theory of Life*", in *Miscellanies, Aesthetic and Literary: To Which is added the Theory of Life* (London: G. Bell and Sons, 1911), 381. Hereafter TL.
55 Owen Barfield, *What Coleridge Thought* (London: Oxford University Press, 1971), 18.
56 TL, 385.
57 Ibid.
58 Coleridge, *Miscellanies*, 19. Italics mine.
59 Barfield summarizes them as follows: '1) absolute dependence of parts and the whole; 2) additional dependence of the whole on parts; 3) greatest number of parts presupposed in whole; 4) parts themselves possessing character of wholes, and this involving their increasing interdependence.' Barfield, *Coleridge*, 51.
60 TL, 379.

abandoning the theoretical inquiry altogether. Coleridge knows that such an argument runs the risk of drifting into an infinite regress but is not ready to completely give up on claiming an (unaccountable) first cause from which life originates. Life can still be 'explained'. The poet excavates the etymological meaning 'explaining' life as a power: 'to explain a power is to unfold and spread it out'.[61] Life is thus observed in its most simple form as an 'instinct' or 'tendency' because it will enable the determination in view of manner and outcome (not origin). This step establishes the condition (not principle) of its possibility and clears up its state with regards to appearance or quality. Positioned in this framework, Coleridge is able to affirm two things: life as a whole will be identified in *kind,* and its unity will be organized by rendering its manifestations as different degrees. 'The tendency been given in *kind*, it is required to tender the phenomena intelligible as its different degrees and modifications'.[62] In a parenthesis, the same thought model is replicated when discussing imagination: the secondary imagination is seen 'as identical with the primary in the kind of its agency, and differing only in degree, and in the mode of operation'.[63]

The reference to the Kantian approach is certainly not a new find in Coleridge's scholarship, and, in this text, we will see how the poet implements the philosopher's pattern of thought in his theory of life and nature.[64] Unlike Fichte's rather subjective and atheistic perspective that starts from the absolute I, Coleridge will opt for a more objective solution. In a nutshell, he carries out Kant's psychological procedures at a cosmological scale turning them into objective laws that derive from a 'self-originating' God. Kant's acts of transcendental apperception involve a self-conscious active subject that overcomes the manifold of intuitions as she holds them together as unity with the aim of presenting this synthesis to understanding and its categories. However, much like Coleridge's presupposed whole, or God, this subjectivity is not an actual subject that knows itself and would, therefore, become able to also posit itself. Like the 'agency' that cannot 'account' for a clearly defined agent, this entity is just a 'transcendental subject' that functions merely as a generic framework that over-watches and merely authorizes the process of understanding. It does not obtain a reflexive status and cannot obtain an identity (like in Fichte), but must still be thought as a necessary condition for the process of cognition. Analogously, Coleridge's God must be presupposed in order for his theory of life to be considered valid.

---

61 TL, 380.
62 Ibid.
63 Fredrick Burwick ed. *Coleridge's Biographia Literaria: Text and Meaning* (Columbus: Ohio State University Press, 1989), 90. Hereafter BL.
64 See for example Gian N. G. Orsini, *Coleridge and German Idealism: A Study in the History of Philosophy* (Carbondale: Southern State Illinois University Press, 1969), 320.

Bearing that in mind, Coleridge still deviates from Kant's philosophy when he endows his divinity with a more active role. Being determined 'to think with and beyond Kant', as Vigus correctly underlines, his attempt to 'explain' this agency pushes it out of a Kantian rather indeterminate position.[65] In doing so, Coleridge's God overcomes a mere natural consciousness as it is brought more (but not fully) into the realm of reflection: it needs to be more than a mere (Spinozian) ground and become an identifiable cause that empowers the unfolding of the created universe.[66] Even though one cannot 'account' for God as the agent behind the creation of the world, one must nonetheless be able to 'presuppose' God as an agency that is not agent-less or impersonal. Unlike Kant, Coleridge handles apperceptive acts of consciousness as acts linked to the conscious will as well. The idea (of life) is a form that turns into 'a mode of action:' 'an instinct or a tendency evident in all its manifestations, and involved in the idea itself'.[67] Coleridge's divinely inspired imagination can, therefore, project its contained unity dissolving, diffusing, dissipating, 'in order to recreate' because God is a 'causative agency' or 'a power, which during its continuance resists or *subordinates* heterogeneous and adverse powers'.[68] One can also note that by not being like Fichte's I, who simply believes it can posit itself absolutely, Coleridge's God would still be able to be 'self-originating' from the perspective of the '*intellectus archetypus*' which is *another form* of intellect according to Kant. Unlike the transcendental subject, the divine can know and have an intuition of Himself directly even if justifying this cognition remains inaccessible to human understanding.

Even though all these "tweaks" collapse Kant's relation between a transcendental subject and an empirical one, Coleridge's thought will still abide by the German philosopher's 'highest principle in the whole sphere of human knowledge' which is the 'principle of apperception'.[69] Even as the unity presupposed by the poet acquires a thetic rather than a hypothetical value, its stable structure remains in place. Coleridge's God will thus obtain an 'infinite power of semination' which allows it to become more efficient than a mere regulative idea

---

65 James Vigus, *The Philosophy of Samuel Taylor Coleridge*, in *The Oxford Handbook of British Philosophy in the Nineteenth Century*, W.J. Mander ed. (London: Oxford University Press, 2014), 532.
66 For more on Coleridge's 'self-originating' rather than 'self-sustaining' God see Richard Berkeley, *Coleridge and the Crisis of Reason* (Hampshire: Palgrave Macmillan, 2007), 95. The critic quotes from *Marginalia:* 'Assuredly, the defect in Spinoza's System is the impersonality of God-he makes his only Substance a *Thing* not a *Will*-a *Ground solely* & at no time a *Cause*'.
67 TL, 380.
68 TL, 371, 372. Italics mine.
69 CPR, B 135, 154.

in an attempt to 'Platonize Kant's account of ideas'.[70] That being said, his God will still retain a numerical identity; the identity of a being that stays the same over time which makes it actually identifiable in kind. Additionally, it still produces representations which are organized sequentially according to forms of intuition. Let us not forget that this causative agency or power (*vis naturans*) [force naturing] is projected in a realm that is 'antecedent' with respect to its creation or *vis naturata* [force natured] as well.[71] The main point is that these changes turn out to be internal and local shifts that do not get to affect the general outlook. The overall framework established by Kant's theory of transcendental apperception still holds, and, from this point of view, Coleridge remains Kantian. Without elaborating on the comparison between Shelley and Coleridge just yet, one can highlight the transcendental apperceptive context and its active role in cognition as a point of contention.

Coleridge's theoretical approach defines life as a relation between the whole's unitary generality and its replication in the particular; in the way it manifests itself in organized beings. More precisely, the causative or creative agency has a double function: it is both the whole or the framework that conveys unity while containing created nature and the 'copula,' (i.e., the verb *is* in a sentence), with respect to the individual part. Coleridge's theory tries to patch up or synthesize two distinct entities: the presupposed and antecedent origin and the connector or the relation. He stages the 'Idea of life' as 'the tendency to individuation' and explains the relation between part and whole as the former's capacity be organized in the same way as the latter. The whole can be recognized in the part according to the degree of organization, according to the way it contains the systematic unity of the whole. The part thus acquires a symbolic quality. However, once the synthesis of apperception organizes the data of the senses, the difference between part and whole becomes specific and 'actual' and not merely 'nominal' anymore. The *principium individuationis* [principle of individuation] structures the part *ab intra* [from inside] as a *forma formans* [forming form] that ends up a *forma formata* [formed form]. It is not a formative principle imposed on a material content from without but comes close to Blumenbach's *Bildungstrieb (vis formativus)* [formative force] or the inborn force in every organism. This

---

70 James Vigus, *Platonic Coleridge* (New York: Modern Humanities Research Association and Routledge, 2009), 168.
71 'This antecedent unity, or cause and principle of each union, it has since the time of Bacon and Kepler been customary to call a law (...) That the root, stem and leaves cohere to one plant, is owning to an antecedent Power or Principle in the Seed which existed before a single particle of the matters (...) has been attracted from the surrounding soil, air, and moisture. Shall we turn to the seed? Here too the same necessity meets us, an antecedent unity (I speak not of the parent plant, but of the agency antecedent in that order of operance (sic), yet remaining present as the conservative and reproductive power) must be supposed'. *On the Prometheus of Aeschylus* in *Miscellanies, Aesthetic and Literary*, 71. Hereafter OPA.

perspective is not far from the Kantian mindset; in his Third Critique, Kant argues for a purposive power (*zweckmässige Macht*) that can be assumed acting in nature as well.[72]

To be more precise, Coleridge observes the procession of life from whole to part as a dialectical process of interaction between opposing forces. The reaction to the tendency to become individualized results in a counter tendency to 'connect' to other parts so as to reconfigure the whole again (i.e., 'the ultimate production of the highest and most comprehensive individuality').[73] This connectivity is based on the degree of consciousness each part carries; it enables them to be 'idealized and unified:' the higher the degree of consciousness embedded in a part, the more likely it is to connect to others and thus to reproduce the systematicity of whole. Coleridge, however, is not just acknowledging the dynamicity of the dialectics of opposing forces but looks to identify it as a law. The law of polarity turns out to be the most general upward oriented, spiraling tendency that is present in nature: 'The tendency having been ascertained, what is its (i.e., nature's) most general law? I answer polarity, or the essential dualism of Nature, arising out of its productive unity, and still tending to reaffirm it, either as equilibrium, indifference, or identity'.[74]

At this point, Coleridge is issuing judgments about nature that could come dangerously close to overstepping the limits of reason. He is not doing this directly or through a mystical communication though; rather by means of analogy. The poet is merely saying that life is composed of two opposites that are analogous to the centripetal and the centrifugal forces. He just 'compares the principle of Life to magnetism, electricity...'.[75] Nature is not a giant magnet that contains two opposite poles. It merely works *as if* it were a magnet that contains those forces. Magnetism is thus analogous to reproduction, electricity analogous to irritability, and chemical process to sensibility. Coleridge distances himself from Abernethy and the vitalist debate knowing that Kant also issued judgments about nature *per analogiam:* reason gives one the right to project a purpose or *telos* in nature.

Analogy presents objects positively as pertaining to appearance. It cannot provide any knowledge on how things exist though. Similarly, the law of polarity cannot be seen to be actually working in nature – the latter would then be turned into an object of cognition with respect to the mind and acknowledge its outside position. It is true that due to his envisaged end (not goal or purpose), Coleridge does conceive the possibility of such an outside position. In a note to *Statesman's*

---

72 For the correspondence between Kant and Blumenbach, see Gigante, 18–21.
73 TL, 392.
74 Ibid.
75 Ibid.

Manual, he takes appropriate precautions though: '...but for the confidence which we place in the assertions of our reason and our conscience, we could have no certainty of the reality and actual outness of the material world'.[76] He cannot be entirely certain because the mind, still in its spiral ascent, has not arrived at that stage in its development where it would become pure consciousness. While the law of polarity remains a valid supposition, it cannot be considered objective: as a rational human being, one can only ascribe a law in nature, and one has the moral duty to act as if this is a continuous progress towards a higher goal.

The propensity of finding such a law can also be credited to the Kantian mindset. It can be traced to Coleridge's engagement with Kant's 'Transcendental Dialectic' that famously restricted the speculative use of reason with respect to the ideas of God, freedom, and immortality to a merely regulative use. The law of polarity unites the human being with nature under one principle, an idea of reason that is superior to the senses. This attempt, however, provides only an intellectual experience (i. e., an experience of ideas of reason), not a sensual one that can be apprehended as an intuition. This experience grants only a form (i. e., the form of a law without a particular implementation), not a content that can be conceptualized. That being said, even if acts are not theorized in view of understanding and remain on an experiential level only, they are still perfectly justified as long as the experience conforms to the law of its possibility: to have an experience at all, the successive data must be combined or held together in a unity for consciousness (i. e., the transcendental unity of apperception.)

It is important to mention that Coleridge's theory of life does not assign a purpose to nature. The fact that life evolves or gradually unveils a higher state of consciousness does not come about due to a *telos*. Rather, it turns out to be a *function* of the law of polarity which he finds throughout creation. The notion of function will not only bring Coleridge closer to Lawrence, but it will also help him 'distinguish her agency from a blind and lifeless mechanism' even 'without assigning to nature as nature, a conscious purpose'.[77] His two main goals were to overcome a mere mechanistic or materialistic view and to establish a unity between the mind and matter. Choosing to introduce the notion of function will keep his theory away from the pantheism of Schelling/Steffens while not subscribing fully to Kant's idealistically assigned purpose as well. Moreover, this shift from psychology to physiology would better safeguard the continuity between the generative powers of *natura naturans* [naturing nature] as it becomes *naturata*, a

---

76 W.G.T. Shedd, ed. *The Complete Works of Samuel Coleridge*, vol. 1 (New York: Harper & Brothers, 1884), 429.
77 *Essay X* in *The Complete Works of Samuel Taylor Coleridge*, vol. 2, (1871), 450.

finite or formed product in which the living power will still act by means of a function.

> The first product of its energy is the thing itself... Still, however, its productive energy is not exhausted in this product, but overflows, or is effluent (sic), as the specific forces, properties, faculties, of the product. It reappears, in short, as the function of the body.[78]

Coleridge opts for a more objective alternative that does not depend entirely on consciousness; a function being an activity or purpose natural to or intended for a person or thing.[79] Raimonda Mondiano summarizes this idea when she affirms that for Coleridge "'I am" becomes "it is"'.[80] Whether Coleridge can truly break out of the psychological context of the *cogito* and truly affirm the *sum* is a different question though.

A function is an objective tendency that can be ascribed to the upwards oriented spiral, which leads to an ever-higher degree of organization. This level is reached by the human mind through its consciousness and thought. Coleridge continues: 'This must be the one great end of Nature, her ultimate object, or by whatever other word we may designate that something which bears to a final cause the same relation that Nature herself bears to the Supreme Intelligence'.[81] This remark is revealing because it could imply a trespassing of the Kantian context: the German thinker has not given any hints that a goal would ever become an end. Without the possibility of being presented as an intuition, the 'one great end of nature' can only be determined as an ideal reference point, a pure possibility without actuality. Human teleology is utterly alien to natural causation and can never explain anything in nature. It will remain merely reflective and can only provide the general idea of causation according to ends because mechanical laws of nature are necessary. The idea of reaching a goal as a rational concept has no constitutive validity. It cannot be considered a principle that could provide knowledge and thus put an end to the infinite progression of our inquiry.

Still, Coleridge affirms the 'great end of Nature' and the real possibility for it to be constituted in experience as an 'ultimate object' of cognition. As Jacob Risinger puts it: 'Coleridge was deeply invested in the process of polarity and its progressive conciliations, but his deepest imaginings looked toward the unity that might mark the end of the process. The power implicit in life was, for Coleridge,

---

78 OPA, 70.
79 Kant also distinguishes objective purpose or purposes that are as much as the subject is able to consider objective.
80 Raimonda Modiano, *Coleridge and the Concept of Nature* (London: Macmillan, 1985), 117.
81 TL, 392.

none other than the "frame of hope".[82] The argument regarding Coleridge's constitutivism has already been made, and the poet himself acknowledges it as well. The question is whether this Platonic 'restoration' would overcome the previously established cognitive premises.[83] Whether constitutive or regulative, whether fully formed and graspable as a concept or merely posited as a maxim or goal, an object of cognition must be declared an object of possible experience first. Objects of possible experience subordinate difference to a principle of identity and are constructed at the outset as representations (*Vorstellungen*). Keeping this in mind, Deleuze argues that both positions cater to the same paradigm of thought because these objects probe first the possibility of how 'the given is given to a subject'.[84] In both cases, knowledge turns out to be the result of previous conditioning because it depends on apperception and the transcendental subject, and, from this perspective, Deleuze will conclude that Kant is 'more Platonic than he thinks'.[85] In addition, from a representative point of view, Coleridge's worldview overcomes inner contradictions, and secures a certain coherence, unity and systematicity.

Coleridge may not follow Kant to the letter, but still when he makes amends to Kant's thought content, he does not overthrow Kant's main cognitive tenet. Vigus puts it eloquently: 'He thus characteristically makes far more explicit assertions of the truth (of Christianity) than Kant would ever allow, but nevertheless from a Kantian basis'.[86] His innovative exercise can be described as a move towards a theory of nature that stays away from regulative goals but cannot fully constitute its ends: 'the one great end of Nature'.[87] The object of cognition is still projected in the future which leaves a margin for error before 'the end' can be fully constituted as a concept. On the one side, the poet is convinced that he has more leverage to argue it after "tinkering" with Kant's regulative aspect, but, on the other, his position still remains skeptical since the 'end' is not 'nigh.' Paul Hamilton is inclined to see it as a mere 'religious consolation' and argues that such 'self-

---

82 Jacob Risinger, 'Coleridge, Politics, and the Theory of Life' in *Sel: Studies in English Literature 1500–1900*, vol. 55, n. 3 (Baltimore: Johns Hopkins University Press, 2015): 665.
83 For more details, see James Vigus, *Platonic Coleridge*.
84 Gilles Deleuze and Constantin V. Boundas trans. introd. *Empiricism and Subjectivity* (New York: Columbia University Press. 1991), 87.
85 Gilles Deleuze and Paul Patton trans. *Difference and Repetition* (New York: Continuum, 1994), 196. Hereafter DR. For the same reason, Plato becomes Kantian. 'The model of recognition is necessarily included in the image of thought, and whether one considers Plato's Theaetetus, Descartes's Meditations, or Kant's *Critique of Pure Reason*, this model remains sovereign and defines the orientation of the philosophical analysis of what it means to think.' DR. 134.
86 Vigus, *Philosophy*, 534.
87 TL. 392.

knowledge was a vanishing point, an ideal convergence never to be achieved'.[88] Again, Vigus also argues that 'Coleridgean ideals are practical in the sense of being at least "approximately" realizable; they are also practical in the Kantian sense of being founded on a moral consciousness, or conscience'.[89]

This essay intends to just map out formal differences between Coleridge and Shelley. It will not articulate a right and wrong judgment even as Coleridge will urge elsewhere 'to find a ground that is unconditional and absolute'.[90] We remember that both Coleridge and Shelley argue for a causal relation with coverage in nature. That said, neither can provide assurance and affirm with certainty to have produced an actual effect or to have grasped an object (or reached an end). The analysis can merely evaluate their attempts while measuring their effectiveness and the question would be the following: which of the two scenarios is more likely to achieve the reality of a future fulfilment? Is it Coleridge's 'final cause', the arrival of the new intelligence, or rather Shelley's coming of spring?

3. Comparative Remarks

Going back to the relationship between whole and part, one can notice an essential difference between Shelley and Coleridge. Shelley's concept of the whole will never acknowledge a dichotomy with its parts. Any modifications to the whole remain merely nominal and expressed in language only: words like 'I, you, they' are just 'grammatical devices' or 'merely an affair of words' that mark just 'modifications of the one mind'.[91] These modifications do not become 'actual' in view of the world of natural things that exist. Thinking as it is expressed in language will therefore dwell merely on itself rather than trying to cross over and comprehend the world.[92] It does not deal with accidents of history or various modes of *relating* to things in nature but stays distant from (yet parallel to) the

---

88 Paul Hamilton, *Coleridge and German Philosophy. The Poet in The Land of Logic* (New York: Continuum, 2007), 54.
89 Vigus, *Philosophy,* 533.
90 'The Friend' in *The Collected Works of Samuel Taylor Coleridge,* ed. Barbara E. Rooke, vol. 4, I (Princeton: Princeton University Press, 1969), 416. Christoph Bode will make the argument that his principles are 'systematically incompatible.' See Fredrick Burwick ed. *Coleridge and Philosophy* in *The Oxford Handbook of Coleridge* (Oxford: Oxford University Press, 2009), 588–619.
91 OL, 542.
92 'For language is arbitrarily produced by the imagination and has relation to thoughts alone'. DP, 563. This aspect is reminiscent also of Hamann's objection to Kant's approach, an issue that has been analyzed by Benjamin. It is also central for Clayton Koelb's approach that finds intriguing similarities between Kant's Third Critique and Hamann. (Koelb, ch.1) This is also its jurisdiction that cannot be crossed without stepping into superstition (*Schwärmerei*).

world: words can name things and establish a nominal/non-actual difference between them but cannot provide any ontological information on them.

When Shelley's all-inclusive whole is perceived as a matter of degrees and intensity of power, it lacks identifying elements and turns out to be just a 'mass of capabilities.' Shelley famously rejected a personalized 'creative deity', while letting 'the hypothesis of pervading spirit co-eternal with the universe remain unshaken.' His idea of divinity is not able to accommodate any formative or structuring principle because Shelley is fully aware of the 'vanity' that seeks to 'discover the formal principle'. As a matter of fact, the vital power behind any act or development remains substantially the same while its structure or a plan through which it manifests itself will *necessarily* change. When an idea from Goethe's *Faust* will furnish the germ and inspiration for future poems, the procession from the originating principle to the fully created object 'is as different from it in structure and plan as the acorn from the oak'.[93]

The effect will, therefore, not have the same form or structure, plan or framework as the cause; their continuity implies change or transformation. Such a substantial wholeness 'remains at every period materially the same' while 'circumstances which awaken into action perpetually change'.[94] Sir William Lawrence would say that 'we see continuous change so that the body cannot be called the same in two successive instants'.[95] The acorn becomes an oak without imprinting its structure, its form *in* it in the same way as the idea (of *Faust*) is a form that does not become formative or *formans*. Involving difference as a necessary element indicates that the product does not come to pass because of a previously established framework of conditions. His notion of creativity would, therefore, be defined as 'expressive' rather than a 'representative'.[96]

Shelley also uses the image of the acorn as a primordial 'first acorn' that contains 'potentially all oaks.' While he rejects God as a Creator, he still does not exclude the existence of the 'mind of the creator.' This mind, however, is an 'image' that merely gathers and comprises 'all other minds' without distinguishing a principle of organization, a structure that could be recognized and thus personalized. As a consequence, it cannot be clearly separated and considered 'antecedent' with respect to creation as well. It remains rather dissipated yet always already contained in it. Shelley adheres consistently to his all-inclusive

---

93 Frederick L. Jones ed. *The Letters*, vol. 2, 407. The same can be said about the transformation from the tree into a guitar.
94 *Preface to Prometheus Unbound*, in *Percy Shelley. Selected Poems and Prose*, 177.
95 William Lawrence, *An Introduction to Comparative Anatomy and Psychology: being the Two Introductory Lectures, delivered at the Royal College of Surgeons on the 21st and 25th of March, 1816* (London: J. Callow, 1819), 139.
96 It is true that Deleuze's concept of representation refers primarily to Aristotle, but it has ties to Kant's *Vorstellung* as well. DR 35.

notion of whole as a 'unsculptured image' that prevents him from 'deifying the principle of the universe'.[97]

Another feature that sets the two poets apart is the fact that even though Coleridge's presupposed transcendental 'causative agency' will also lack a precise determination – one cannot 'account' for it as a personalized God – it will still act like an eminence that enables life while watching over creation's process of becoming as well. This entity is still determinable *a priori*. Even if one cannot have a (sensual) experience of Him, Coleridge's God does not overstep the conditions of possibility of having one. In a parenthesis, one can say that this aspect calls to mind Deleuze's critique of Duns Scotus: the latter's concept of God is played out as a relation between 'a generic difference and a specific difference'.[98] The predicates are just opposed (the law of polarity), and difference in itself cannot be achieved while God, the principle of life, remains without any 'sense of being'.[99] As this concept of whole turns out to be a totalizing whole – its totality being composed (*zusammengesetzt*) of parts – concerns can be raised with respect to the efficiency of the imagination that is supposed to 'vitalize' or 'revivify' by 'recreating' what Coleridge calls 'the ultimate production of the highest and most comprehensive individuality'.[100]

In a scenario where one cannot even presuppose a 'causative agency,' a condition of possibility that would allow mounting a rational argument which provides knowledge and 'explain' the world of things as an effect of such an agency, the mind or reason becomes unable to project or *actively* construct the world by means of imagination and will, therefore, be bound to 'only perceive' and render 'passively': 'the everlasting universe of things' will 'flow through the mind' and end up 'governing thought'.[101] The faculty of imagination will then get to exercise its *poietic* ability by being able to immediately experience and process sensations and only subsequently present its results to reason. The mind itself becomes a mystery as well, and Shelley merely deduces its properties from experience; any *a priori* information would by default give priority to the mind over

---

97 *Notes on Queen Mab* in *Percy Shelley. Selected Poems and Prose*, 93.
98 DR, 303.
99 Deleuze concludes that the 'analogy of being' will miss both extremities, both the whole and the part, both God and created things: 'what is missed at the two extremities is a sense of being and the play of individuating difference in being. Everything takes place between generic difference and specific difference. The genuine universal is missed no less than the true singular.' Ibid.
100 TL, 392. Kant's concept of composition is fundamental in the process of thinking. The synthetic unity of apperception is based on composing the data given to the senses (i.e., the Humean 'mere heap' of impressions or the 'chaos of sensations'). While analyzing Hamann's approach, Clayton Koelb brings Section 49 of the Third Critique where Kant also discusses the 'animating principle' (*belebende Prinzip*) of the mind. see Koelb, 14.
101 'Mont Blanc' in *Selected Poems*, 138.

life. 'Mind, as far as we have any experience of its properties, and beyond that experience how vain is argument! cannot create, it can only perceive'.[102]

Shelley's idea of passivity is essential in the way he theorizes the poetic process as well. As an 'expression of the imagination,' poetry must be distinguished from reasoning, because the latter is 'a power to be exerted according to the determination of the *will*. A man cannot say, "I will compose poetry"'.[103] Poetic power thus arises 'from within,' entirely on its own and the 'conscious portions of our natures are unprophetic either of its approach or its departure.' By comparison, Coleridge, already in 1801, 'rejected the idea of the mind as a "lazy looker-on on the external world".[104] Later, it becomes 'a mirror reflecting the landscape, or, as blank canvas upon which some unknown hand paints it' or, 'the mere quicksilver plating behind a looking-glass!'.[105] For him, the poetical ability resides in the use of the secondary imagination which is 'co-existing with the conscious will.' His imaginative power is 'first put in action by the will and understanding, and retained under their irremissible, though gentle and unnoticed, *control*'.[106] When placed under such transcendental over-watch, imagination is no longer in 'first and original' position and its freedom becomes restricted. Even if this controlling authority acts merely as a remote framework that remains unnoticed, vague, or evanescent, it is still a necessary component and will impact the poetic process. Finally, the active position of the mind is a consequence of Coleridge's subscribing to a transcendental apperceptive context.

Drawing closer to a conclusion, one will say that the difference between the two poets is no longer a formal one, a difference of degree like the previously mentioned certainty of a future fulfilment. The opposition would record their difference as specific while pertaining to a general class or genus. However, when perception is taken over by transcendental apperception, the whole context changes. Everything needs to be re-written according to the requirements of a new type of unity: intensive magnitudes become inadmissible as they are perceived and demand to be reevaluated and further processed. They end up being organized according to a principle that is alien to their nature in such a way that, when looked at, they can only be 'anticipated.' This hiatus prevents establishing a relation between the two contexts based on an overarching law or principle; the

---

102 OL, 542.
103 DP, 575.Italics mine.
104 E. L. Griggs, ed. *Collected Letters of Samuel Coleridge* vol. 1 (Oxford: Oxford University Press 1956-71), 177. Even though he later tried to retract the content of the letter, C.U.M. Smith believes that one can still make the case that it is one of his enduring opinions. See 'Coleridge's "Theory of Life"' in *Journal of the History of Biology,* vol.32, No. 1 (Spring 1999): 37.
105 BL, I, 66, ch. V and BL, I, 82, ch. VII.
106 BL, I, ch. XIV. Italics mine.

opposition pertains to particular aspects only. This incompatibility not only accounts for some of their "creative differences" but makes a comparison between the two romantic poets impossible.

4. Conclusion

The fact that ideas by the two poets have been found to pertain to separate systems of thought which cannot function under the same principle forbids a comparison. This finding submits a break that reaches beyond a (static or finite) contradiction which still presupposes a common measure; contrasting and antithetical is different from incompatible and divergent. A link between the two poets will then have to summon an infinite yet dynamic perspective: only an all-inclusive whole would be able to reconcile both as 'modifications', albeit of a different type. While the nature of such bond would have to be analyzed elsewhere, one can presently say that even if one side is assessed as an 'error,' it still remains relevant in view of a learning process, in view of an 'education.' *Mutatis mutandis,* [having changed what needs to be changed] but similar to the way, Hegel learned from Kant while including him in the spirit's historical becoming, this dialogic analysis hopes to have highlighted some of the intricacies of a labyrinthine and multifaceted movement.[107]

---

[107] Sally West argues for a 'true dialog' when she says: 'His (Shelley's) engagement with Coleridge had progressed from imitation to criticism to a true dialog where the concerns of the elder poet's works are explored and elaborated upon as part of Shelley's own developing vision.' Sally West, *Coleridge and Shelley. Textual Engagement* (New Hampshire: Ashgate, 2007), 175.

Jørgen Huggler
(Aarhus University)

Democracy, General Will, and Political Formation. Friedrich Schlegel's Critique and Reconstruction of the Concept of 'Republicanism'

Abstract
Friedrich Schlegel's critique of Immanuel Kant's claim that democracy is necessarily despotic (as in ancient Greece, lacking a strict separation between legislative and executive power) led Schlegel to formulate an alternative concept of democracy, opposing republicanism and despotism. His alternative understanding led him to a new notion of the Rousseauian distinction (and relation) between general will and the will of the majority, and to seek new paths to a realization of the project of perpetual peace, viz. through political and historical formation. Schlegel's aim is to bridge the gap between a priori principles and anthropological and empirical reality.

Keywords
Friedrich Schlegel, Political legitimacy, General will, Democracy, Political formation

Introduction

Immanuel Kant's treatise *Zum ewigen Frieden: Ein philosophischer Entwurf* [Toward Perpetual Peace: A Philosophical Sketch] from 1795 was immediately translated into French, English, Polish, and Danish. It occasioned many critiques and replies, published in French, German, and Swedish journals.[1] Among these is a French critique by Ludwig Ferdinand Huber linking Kant's philosophical revolution with the French Revolution. Johann Gottlieb Fichte, Friedrich Schlegel, Benjamin Höijer (in Swedish), Friedrich Wilhelm von Schütz, Joseph Görres,

---

1 Cf. the bibliography in Immanuel Kant, *Über den Gemeinspruch: Das mag in der Theorie richtig sein, taugt aber nicht für die Praxis* & *Zum ewigen Frieden. Ein philosophischer Entwurf*, ed. Heiner F. Klemme (Hamburg: Felix Meiner Verlag, 1992), LXVIII f. References to these two texts follow the pagination in *Kants gesammelte Schriften*, Hrsg. von der Königlich Preußischen Akademie der Wissenschaften, Bd. VIII, ed. Heinrich Maier (Berlin: De Gruyter, 1923) [*Ak*.]. On Schlegel-quotations, cf. note 3. Unless otherwise noted, all translations are my own.

and Friedrich von Gentz wrote prominent replies.[2] I will here present and examine Friedrich Schlegel's contribution in its own right.

In the essay 'Versuch über den Begriff des Republikanismus' [Essay on the Concept of Republicanism] from 1796, Friedrich Schlegel presents a critique and reconstruction of the concept of 'republicanism' in Immanuel Kant's treatise.[3] Over the last decade, some readers of Schlegel's text have considered an aesthetic agenda to take precedence over the political reasoning it contains. Undoubtedly, this has helped distance Schlegel from French Jacobinism and helped in understanding his later political development and support of Roman Catholicism and the Austrian Empire.[4] Nevertheless, the revolution in France and subsequent European developments seem to provide an obvious backdrop for Schlegel's highly diverse writings on history and politics.[5] Another important strand of interpretation was shaped recently by interest in the history and diversity of cosmopolitanism, inspired by Immanuel Kant.[6]

Schlegel opposes with strong arguments the Kantian distinction between republicanism and democracy. Instead, he argues quite convincingly for a more important distinction between republicanism and despotism. His critique of Kant's so-called guarantee of progress toward perpetual peace is enlightening and unveils an obvious and convincing alternative approach, *viz.* the importance of communication, of historical political experience, and of 'politische Bildung' [political formation] – aspects missing from Kant's project. The general discussion of republicanism in opposition to despotism leads him to reconsider ancient republics. It also implies a more restricted alternative to Kant's peace project and leads to a different answer to the question of insurrection, so vehe-

---

2 A collection of 13 reviews and replies from the period 1796–1800 is reprinted in Immanuel Kant, *Zum ewigen Frieden. Ein philosophischer Entwurf. Texte zur Rezeption 1796–1800*, eds. Manfred Buhr and Steffen Dietzsch (Leipzig: Verlag Philipp Reclam jun., 1984).

3 Friedrich Schlegel, 'Versuch über den Begriff des Republikanismus veranlaßt durch die Kantische Schrift zum ewigen Frieden' (1796), in *Kritische Friedrich-Schlegel-Ausgabe* [KA], Hrsg. Ernst Behler unter Mitwirkung von Jean-Jacques Anstett und Hans Eichner (Paderborn etc.: Verlag Ferdinand Schöningh, 1958ff.), Bd. VII (1966), 11–25. Engl. transl.: 'Essay on the Concept of Republicanism occasioned by the Kantian tract "Perpetual Peace"', in *The Early Political Writings of the German Romantics* [PW], ed. Frederick C. Beiser (Cambridge: Cambridge University Press, 1996), 93–112, doi: 10.1017/cbo9781139170604. – Schlegel-quotations, where the references begin with 'Schlegel, PW', are from Beiser's translation.

4 Cf. e.g. Peter D. Krause, '"Vollkommne Republik". Friedrich Schlegels frühe politische Romantik', *Internationales Archiv für Sozialgeschichte der deutschen Literatur* 27.1 (2002): 1–31, doi: 10.1515/iasl.2002.1.1.

5 Cf. Matthias Schöning, 'Geschichte und Politik', in *Friedrich Schlegel Handbuch. Leben-Werk-Wirkung*, ed. Johannes Endres (Stuttgart: J. B. Metzler Verlag, 2017), 238–263, doi: 10.1007/978-3-476-05370-1_55. This is a very informative contribution focusing on the relevant texts and their contexts.

6 Cf. Pauline Kleingeld, *Kant and Cosmopolitanism. The Philosophical Ideal of World Citizenship* (Cambridge: Cambridge University Press, 2012), doi: 10.1017/cbo9781139015486.

mently denied by Kant due to the structure of political autonomy in a political social contract (being a *pactum unionis*, in contrast to a feudal *pactum subjectionis*).⁷ Opposing Kant, the thinker of political continuity as a condition for the rule of law, Schlegel presents historically well-informed reflections on the beginning and the end of political legitimacy. Dictatorship can be legitimate: states of emergency *do* exist in reality. However, the defeat of constitutionalism allows for other solutions than those offered by Kant – it allows for rebellion.

In the following, I will explore Schlegel's inventive contribution to political philosophy as expressed in the aforementioned essay from 1796. My focus will be on Schlegel's reference to the institutions of ancient Athenian democracy, and on his original contribution to a development of Jean-Jacques Rousseau's concept of *volonté générale* [general will].⁸ Schlegel points to the various degrees of realization of republicanism, and to moral and political formation – an aspect neglected by Kant, although immensely important, in Schlegel's view, for the development of mankind – as a condition for the development of full republicanism. An alliance of republics in a 'Friedensbund' [a federation of peace] presupposes some threat from belligerent, despotic states.⁹ This implies a culture-dependent approach to everlasting peace, restricted to republican fraternity and to the phenomenon of *isonomia* [equal rights], as it was known among city-states in antiquity, distinct from Kant's universalism.¹⁰

Here, Schlegel, the most ardent proponent of classical history, literature, and philosophy in early German romanticism, challenges Kantian political rationalism – partly through its own (perhaps inconsistent) reasoning, partly through a historical understanding of antiquity divergent from Kant's and partly through a new understanding of Rousseauian principles of political legitimacy. In doing so, Schlegel makes an important contribution to the question of democratic will formation and of education for a democratic rule of law.

Thus, Schlegel's reading of Kant's treatise *Toward Perpetual Peace* leads to an interesting discussion of Rousseau's problematic concept 'general will'. Schlegel makes a strong case for the concept as a first principle of political legitimacy. In a highly consistent manner, Schlegel deals with general will as the

---

7 Cf. Ingeborg Mauss, *Zur Aufklärung der Demokratietheorie. Rechts- und demokratietheoretische Überlegungen im Anschluß an Kant* (Frankfurt am Main: Suhrkamp, 1992).
8 Jean-Jacques Rousseau, *Du Contrat social*, ed. Pierre Burgelin (Paris: Flammarion, 1966), 52. (Livre I, Ch. 6).
9 Schlegel, KA VII, 22; PW 108.
10 'Equality' (íson) has be called 'die Grundidee der Demokratie' [the basic idea of democracy], cf. Jochen Bleicken, *Die athenische Demokratie* (Paderborn: Ferdinand Schöningh, 1995), 46. 'Isonomía' means equal political right, or equal share in nómos), ibid. 66. An example of this use is Plato, *The Republic*, 563b. Nevertheless, the relation between 'isonomía' (a term used already by Herodotus) and 'democracy' is still an issue for philological and philosophical debate.

Fig. 1: Title page of Jean-Jacques Rousseau, *Principes du droit politique*, 1762.

normative foundation of republicanism. With his own concept of 'juridical fiction', Schlegel suggests a solution to the problem of how to reconcile general will in its normativity and *a priori* character with the empirical decisions made by the people or their representatives.[11] In contrast to Kant's appeal to nature, Schlegel appeals to culture and political experience and formation in order to make the world more peaceful.

---

11 In contrast to Schlegel, Rousseau held that the legislative sovereignty of the general will can never be alienated, nor can it be *represented*, cf. *Du Contrat social*, 63 (Livre II, Ch. 1.). Rousseau, however, admits that the executive forms of government may vary from democracy over aristocracy to monarchy, ibid. 105 (Livre III, Ch. 3). He even admits that mixed government can be a remedy, when the executive power is not sufficiently dependent on the legislative, ibid. 116f. (Livre III, Ch. 7).

Schlegel's Criticism of Kant's Distinction between Republicanism and Democracy

According to Kant's *Zum ewigen Frieden* (1795), *republicanism* and *democracy* are incompatible. In this work, Kant claimed the universality of 'republicanism', by which he understood states ruled by laws that, due to their universality, were in principle acceptable to every citizen. Republicanism is an institution that is a necessary positive prescription (a definitive article) for achieving perpetual peace.[12] In contrast, Kant considered 'democracy', as found in ancient Greece and Rome, to be a form of despotism because it did not distinguish between legislative and executive power, and therefore did not protect minorities against a 'general will', which, by excluding the acceptance of such minorities, was not general at all but merely the will of a numeric majority.

Against Kant's contention that a republic will degrade into despotism if *executive* power is not kept separate from *legislative* power, Schlegel objects, firstly, that despotism could also involve a strict division of political powers and, secondly, that an exceptional acceptance of transitory dictatorship could be a legitimate decision made by the people in a republic. Against Kant's conceptions of the Attic democracy, Schlegel underlines that ancient republics in fact had representative organs, and that even transitory dictatorship was a mode of representation in a republic, although an exceptional one, as documented in ancient history.[13] It is a particular sort of representation, strictly limited to a temporary and short-lived existence. It is legitimized in cases where it represents a surrogate for the general will. Presumably, Schlegel did not fear that such a dictatorship would destroy the distinction between executive, legislative, and juridical powers. His references point to ancient Greece and Rome. By contrast, the concept of a *dictatura perpetua* [a perpetual dictatorship] is a contradiction in terms and incompatible with the idea of a constitution.[14]

---

12 Kant's treatise distinguishes between (negative) 'Preliminary Artices' and (positive) 'Definitive Articles'. The six 'Preliminary Articles' forbid: 1. secret reservations in peace treaties, and 2. states to become dominated by other states, 3. standing armies, 4. accumulation of national debts, 5. interference by force with the constitution of another state, 6. or to permit acts of hostility which would make mutual confidence in peace impossible in future (Kant, *Ak.* 343–348). The three 'Definitive Articles' provide a foundation for a future peace. These are: 1. The *constitutional law* of every state should be *republican*. 2. The *law of nations* should be founded on a *federation of free states*. 3. The *law of world citizenship* shall be *limited* to conditions of universal hospitality (Kant, *Ak.* 348–360). – For a detailed analysis of Kant's treatise, cf. Jørgen Huggler, 'Cosmopolitanism and Peace in Kant's Essay on Perpetual Peace', *Studies in Philosophy and Education* 29 (2010): 129–140, doi: 10.1007/s11217-009-9167-x.
13 For a discussion of Kant's understanding, cf. Ulrich Thiele, 'Demokratischer Pazifismus. Aktuelle Interpretationen des ersten Definitivartikels der Kantischen Friedensschrift', *Kant-Studien* 99.2 (2008): 180–199, doi: 10.1515/kant.2008.012.
14 Schlegel, KA VII, 14 & 18; PW 99 & 104.

Schlegel's article is thus a criticism of the Kantian distinction between republicanism and democracy. Kant held republicanism to be a particular type of *constitution*, characterized by its reverence for freedom and equality. Against this, Schlegel regards *freedom* and *equality* as fundamental features of *every* constitution. Therefore, these features cannot be used without circularity as a distinctive, defining characteristic of what is called a *republican* constitution.[15] As different forms of state, not of constitution, the more important distinction should be made between republicanism and despotism.

Schlegel bases his reasoning on an analysis that seems to be inspired by Jean-Jacques Rousseau's distinction between the 'volonté générale' [the general will] and the 'volonté de tous' [the will of all] in *Du Contrat social* [The Social Contract] (1762).[16] Schlegel conceives of the general will as a normative *a priori* principle.[17] By contrast, he conceives of the will of all, or the will of the many – or, more correctly, in Schlegel's own wording, 'der Wille der Mehrheit' [the will of the majority] – as an empirical collective result of the – in strength and orientation – potentially divergent political wills representing the people.[18] 'Der politische Imperativ' [the political normativity] in a society that aims at a community of humanity, called a 'Staat' [state], is based on political liberty and political equality, thus demanding that general will should be the foundation of every individual political activity, be it an expression of legislative, judicial, or executive power.[19]

Aiming at such accordance with general will is the defining characteristic of republicanism, although this idea may be realized to different degrees.

Thus, Schlegel underlines the fundamental opposition between republicanism and despotism. Despotism, built on private will and aiming at particular ends, can only potentially develop into a state. As a principle for distinction, only the number of rulers (tyranny, oligarchy, ochlocracy; see below) can be used if private will, i.e., despotism, rather than general will, decides civic legislation. However, because the general will as an *a priori* principle is not, and cannot be, an empirical phenomenon, republics need the *fiction* of an empirical will that acts *according to* general will in order to perform the political imperative. Therefore, the will of the majority has to be considered a surrogate for the general will. Schlegel says, in contrast to Kant: 'thus, Republicanism is necessarily democratic'.[20] Kant's paradox that democracy must be despotic cannot be right, Schlegel adds.[21]

---

15 Schlegel, KA VII 11f.; PW 95f.
16 Rousseau, *Du Contrat social*, 66 (Livre II, Ch. 3).
17 Schlegel, KA VII, 14 & 16; PW 98f. & 101.
18 Schlegel, KA VII, 17; PW 102.
19 Schlegel, KA VII, 15; PW 100.
20 'Der Republikanismus ist also notwendig demokratisch', Schlegel, KA VII, 17; PW 102.
21 Ibid.

Schlegel's alternative Conceptions and his Reasons

In regard to the defence of freedom and equality: according to Schlegel, Kant has not outlined any principles for his differentiation of the types and elements of states. Instead, Schlegel offers a *'deduction of republicanism* and a *political classification a priori'*, based on his conception of normativity.[22] He understands the political imperative as a specific modification of what he calls 'the pure practical imperative'.[23] The pure practical imperative is modified in relation to the theoretical datum of different human 'Vermögen' [capabilities].[24] This has implications for Schlegel's option for formation: in relation to other individuals of the human kind, the person has 'das Vermögen der Mitteilung' [the capacity of communication].[25] Individuals have mutual relations of dependency and communication. Thus, the assertion 'Gemeinschaft der Menschheit soll sein, oder das Ich soll mitgeteilt werden' ['the community of humanity should be' or 'the ego should be communicated'] can be derived from the more basic sentence: 'Das Ich soll sein' ['the ego should be'].[26] The derivative practical assertion of the demand for community of mankind and of communication is, according to Schlegel, the foundation and the object of *Politics*. Politics, he states, is here not understood as the Kantian concept of politics as *an art* to make the mechanisms of nature useful for ruling men. Instead, politics according to Schlegel should, on a par with ancient Greek philosophical conceptions, be understood as 'eine praktische Wissenschaft' [a practical discipline] that concerns the relation between practical, i. e., acting, individuals.[27]

---

22 Schlegel, KA VII, 14; PW 99.
23 Ibid.
24 Ibid.
25 Schlegel, KA VII, 14; PW 100.
26 Schlegel, KA VII, 15; PW 100.
27 Ibid. Friederike Rese, in her study, 'Republikanismus, Geselligkeit und Bildung. Zu Friedrich Schlegels "Versuch über den Begriff des Republikanismus"', *Athenäum* 7 (1997): 37–71, defends the assertion that the Schlegelian 'The ego should be' implies the demand for a human being to take care of his own 'Bildung' [formation], transforming himself from an empirical person and attempting to approximate the pure 'I'. Rese reconstructs what Schlegel may have meant by *Bildung* with references to J.G. Fichte and to A.L. Hülsen, and to other texts by Schlegel himself. Then she considers by which features society can make *Bildung* possible. Her analysis is certainly very helpful because Schlegel's presentation of *Bildung* in his essay only consists of a few words, and because she traces the implications as far as to Schlegel's concept of 'Symphilosophie'. Nevertheless, in his essay, Schlegel clearly speaks of 'political Bildung'. To deduce freedom and equality as transcendental conditions for individual *Bildung* through 'Gespräch' [communication], as Rese does (pp. 45–52) in a Kantian sense of 'deduction' (understood as the answer to a *questio juris*), seems to reverse the order of the argument. Schlegel (cf. KA VII, 12) uses a Fichtean model of deduction, formulating a basic sentence and then asking which derivative assertions (and which limitations of these assertions) the sentence demands.

Every 'Gesellschaft' [society] that aims for the 'Gemeinschaft der Menschheit' [community of mankind] is called a 'Staat' [state], Schlegel adds. Now, because 'das Ich' [the ego] 'should be', not only in the relation between all individuals but also in every *single* individual, every person should claim an independent will.[28] As such, political *freedom* is a necessary condition for the political imperative and a defining feature of the concept of state.[29] A denial would contradict the basic, pure, practical imperative from which both the ethical and the political imperative are derived. In addition, these imperatives do not only have validity for this or that individual, but for *every* individual.[30] Thus, political *equality*, too, is a necessary condition for the political imperative and a defining feature of the concept of state. Schlegel explicitly insisted on the principle of universal 'Stimmrecht' [suffrage] for all, including the poor and women as well as all who were not directly proven to lack free will or to be criminals unable to participate in the general will.[31] Presumptions are, according to Schlegel, not sufficient reasons to deprive persons of their political rights: 'If the political fiction to regard an individual as a *political non-entity* ["eine *politische Null*"], a person as a *thing*, were permitted, then it would thwart the opposite of the arbitrary presupposition [i.e., thwart the free will of all individuals], and so conflict with the ethical imperative, which is impossible, given that both rest on the pure practical imperative'.[32]

The external features of the state and the *political imperative* are limiting conditions for the principle of general will. The political imperative refers to everybody. Thus, the state must include a continuous, coexistent, and successive *mass*, namely the totality of inhabitants within the border of a country, or, as another physical (i.e., not political) criterion, the descendants of the same *tribe*. Referring to such a totality, *states* differ from other associations, which only unite a certain limited group of individuals and seek to promote certain particular interests. Thus, Schlegel maintains, freedom and equality request that the general will be the foundation for every political activity – not only for legislation, but also for judicial and executive power. It is precisely this that is the defining feature of republicanism.[33]

By contrast, despotism, founded only on private will, cannot claim to be a state in a strict sense. It is only a quasi-state, or a defective variety of state, with the external features of a state (i.e., totality and continuity of its members), but

---

28 Schlegel, KA VII, 15; PW 100.
29 Ibid.
30 Ibid.
31 Schlegel, KA VII, 17; PW 102.
32 Schlegel, PW 102f.; KA VII, 17.
33 Schlegel, KA VII, 15; PW 101.

nevertheless not what it should be, merely usurping features of a genuine state and perhaps containing the seed to develop into one.[34]

* * *

Here, we come to Schlegel's resolution of the problem that the general will is not a principle that is realized in the empirical world. The Kantian juridical concepts of freedom and equality, Schlegel argues, are, from a *political* point of view, only *minimal*. Freedom and equality, however, should be conceived as *ideas* to be realized through an infinite progression of approximation.[35] This makes graduation possible in terms of the realization of republics.

Further graduated, the *medium* freedom would be what the represented majority of the people actually have willed and the (imagined) universal people could will. No other inequality than the inequality accepted in this way is legitimized. The *maximum* would be that you could do everything you wanted to do (freedom), and that there would be absolute equality of rights and obligations, which would put an end to political domination and dependency. Such a realization is not impossible in terms of principles. Only empirical facts have determined the current situation, and relations of domination, therefore, do not *per se* define conditions for a political community.[36]

The concept of a juridical fiction of an empirical will that (as an approximation of and 'a surrogate for a general will') acts according to general will in order to

---

34 Schlegel, KA VII, 15f.; PW 101.
35 Schlegel, KA VII, 12; PW 97. According to Schöning, 'Geschichte und Politik', Schlegel attacks Kant's concept of republicanism and Kant's philosophy of history (p. 240). Schöning finds two 'romantic' traits in Schlegel's text, *viz.* his reference to an 'infinite approximation to an idea' and his use of a 'fictio juris'. However, these instances do not offer all the desired support for Schöning's claim. The notion of an infinite approximation to an idea is used in Kant's philosophy of history: 'Nur die Annäherung zu dieser Idee ist uns von der Natur Auferlegt' (Immanuel Kant: 'Idee zu einer allgemeinen Geschichte in weltbürgerlicher Absicht' (1784), Sechster Satz, *Ak.* VIII, 17–31). The concept of a *fictio juris* was, and is, a well-known juridical concept stemming from Roman jurisprudence and meaning an 'as if' extension of the factual case. Consequently, Schlegel's essay seems more a contribution to (mainstream) political philosophy than to a particular *romantic* theory, although it might be found compatible with Schlegel's later ideas of romanticism, for instance the doctrines expressed in his *Athenäum*-Fragment 116. Nevertheless, Schöning is right in assuming a divergence between Schlegel's and Kant's philosophy of history. The difference lies in Kant's attachment to a teleology of nature, whereas Schlegel sticks to the role of freedom (or better the 'Wechselwirkung' [reciprocal action/community] of freedom and nature) in history (Schlegel, KA I, 630). Cf. Ernst Behler, *Unendliche Perfektibilität. Europäische Romantik und Französische Revolution*, Paderborn etc.: Ferdinand Schöningh, 1989), 265–280, who uses this wording from Schlegel's Condorcet critique (*viz. KA*, VII, 8), and traces its forerunners in Schlegel's works on Greek poetry.
36 Schlegel, KA VII, 12f.; PW 97.

perform the political imperative is one of Schlegel's most striking contributions to political theory.[37] A juridical fiction is a device basing a judgment on counterfactual assumptions.[38] Bridging the gap between the *a priori,* normative, general will, defined by its attention to the common good, and the empirical will of the deputies representing the people, 'diese höchste fictio juris' [this highest juridical fiction], as Schlegel adds, reflects, in my view, a clear understanding of the problems of Rousseau's political philosophy, including the problematic path to realizing the social contract.[39] According to Schlegel, the fiction has its legitimacy and validity because it is based on the political imperative and because it is the only way to ensure its realization. More precisely, the fiction is based on the principle of equality, thus making the will of the majority a surrogate for general will.[40]

Schlegel accepts a broad range of forms of representation in republics. Thus, he objects to Kant's understanding, as I explained earlier. According to Schlegel, the republics of ancient Greece and Rome were genuine republics with representative organs that are nowadays seldom understood, *viz.* the system of allocating public offices by lot, short terms of office, etc. However, Schlegel also points to the weak technical organization.[41] Perhaps he is referring to the short duration of the Greek polis culture; cf. his essay on Greek comedy (1794).[42] Nevertheless, the 'Gemeinschaft der Sitten' [the ethical community] and 'politische Bildung' [political formation] in the ancient world were much *more* developed than those of modern societies, Schlegel maintains.[43]

---

37 Schlegel, KA VII, 16; PW 102.
38 Cf. *Friedrich Schlegel – Werke in zwei Bänden*, ed. Wolfgang Hecht (Berlin und Weimar: Aufbau-Verlag 1980), Bd. I, 61 & 326.
39 Cf. Wolfgang Kersting, *Jean-Jacques Rousseaus 'Gesellschaftsvertrag'* (Darmstadt: Wissenschaftliche Buchgesellschaft, 2002), 122ff., about the relation between general will and the will of all, and Frederick Neuhouser, *Rousseau's Theodicy of Self-Love: Evil, Rationality, and the Drive for Recognition* (Oxford: Oxford University Press, 2008), 192ff., doi: 10.1093/acprof:oso/9780199542673.001.0001.
40 Schlegel, KA VII, 17; PW 102. Peter Schnyder, 'Politik und Sprache in der Frühromantik. Zu Friedrich Schlegels Rezeption der Französischen Revolution', *Athenäum* 9 (1999): 39–65, analyzes Schlegel's understanding of communication and the use of language as part of his understanding of politics. Schnyder understands Schlegel's essay on republicanism as an attempt to produce an understanding of the field of discourse of politics. In that attempt, Schlegel understood language and communication as the core issue of politics (Schnyder, p. 46). As such, Schlegel's references to the will of the majority should be taken as a sign of an understanding of democracy much more open to deliberation than Rousseau's fear of a deviation from the general will (Schnyder, p. 50).
41 Schlegel, KA VII, 18: PW 103.
42 Schlegel, 'Vom ästhetischen Werte der griechischen Komödie', KA I, 24f.
43 Schlegel wanted to find his own 'romantic' understanding of, and answers to *la querelle des Anciens et des Modernes,* cf. Behler, *Unendliche Perfektibilität. Europäische Romantik und Französische Revolution,* 271f. This seems to be a core issue in Schlegel's early studies. Unfortunately, his essay *Ueber antiken und modernen Republiken* (1795) has been lost.

In fact, these ancient organs had their foundation in a valid fiction concerning the totality as represented through the majority. No subsequent state has developed more 'Gemeinschaft' [community], more freedom, and more equality than Attica.[44] The principle of representation was known in Athens and in republican Rome as well. The people of Attica could not carry out executive power in person, and in Rome, some of the legislative and judicial power was bestowed on representatives of the people.[45]

Political power, according to Schlegel, is an expression of the force of the majority, as 'an approximation to universality ["Allheit", i.e., all the people] and as a surrogate of the general will'.[46] In order to *classify* political phenomena as expressions of this power, Schlegel distinguishes between permanent and transitory features. 'Die Konstitution' [the constitution] encompasses the permanent features of political power and its main elements, whereas 'die Regierung' [the government] encompasses the transitory expressions of political power. In principle, the constitutional power is dictatorial because it cannot depend upon the political functions that depend upon the constitution, *viz.* the legislative, the judicial, and the executive power. However, having founded the constitution, this dictatorial power is also vanishing, because it needs acceptance. Political power, i.e., the majority of the people, must be represented, Schlegel claims.[47]

The constitution in republics refers, on the one hand, to a form of fiction (the surrogate for general will); on the other hand, it refers to a divergent variety of mixed forms of representation between an aristocratic and a democratic orientation.[48]

Despotism, by contrast, cannot be classified in relation to a political constitution. Due to the circumstance that its constitution is only physical (i.e., geographical, not political), it has to be classified according to a mathematical

---

44 'das attische Volk' – an emendation for *britische* (Schlegel, KA VII, 18), suggested by Wolfgang Hecht in *Friedrich Schlegel – Werke in zwei Bänden*, Bd. I, 64 & 327. Also followed by Beiser in Schlegel, PW 103.
45 Schlegel, KA VII 18; PW 104.
46 Schlegel, PW 104; KA VII 18.
47 Schlegel, KA VII, 18; PW 104.
48 Schlegel, KA VII, 19; PW 104f. Schlegel's thought seems to be in analogy to Rousseau's notion of a 'législateur' in *Du Contrat social*, 76ff. (Livre II, Ch. 7), referring back to the mythic founding legislators of Ancient Greek *poleis*, such as Lycurgus who made the institutions of Sparta. Rousseau writes (ibid., 77): 'At the birth of societies, says Montesquieu, it is the chiefs of republics who make the institution, and after that it is the institutions that form the chiefs of republics' (Rousseau, '*The Social Contract*' *and other later political writings*, trs. Victor Gourevitch (Cambridge: Cambridge University Press, 1997), 69), doi: 10.1017/9781316584 606. Aristotle discusses the problems concerned with states designed by such lawgivers as Lycurgus, Solon, etc., in the second book of his *Politics*.

principle, counting the numeric quantity of the persons in charge.⁴⁹ As such, Schlegel distinguishes between tyrannical, oligarchic, and ochlocratic, despotic rules which have an individual, an estate (or caste), or a mob as ruler. Ochlocracy is a despotic rule of the majority over the minority. In contrast to republican democracy, it is defined by the majority being in clear disagreement with the general will – for which it (from the republican point of view) ought to have been a surrogate. Besides tyranny, ochlocracy is 'das größte physische Übel' [the greatest physical evil].⁵⁰ Schlegel – in the spring of 1796 – was certainly no admirer of French Jacobinism, but, nevertheless, he found that 'the Neroes of the world could easily compete with Sansculottism'.⁵¹ Thus, as seen in oriental caste systems and in European feudalism, oligarchy, due to its 'colossal solidity' and its vigilance, and the elite's *esprit de corps*, is an even greater danger to humanity and development. It is of longer duration than the 'uncaring monster' of tyranny.⁵²

To sum up: Schlegel's 'deduction of republicanism' is based on the political imperative, as is his 'classification' of political forms. The republican state has to be valued in respect to its varying amount of 'Gemeinschaft' [community], freedom, and equality.⁵³

---

49 Schlegel, KA VII, 19; PW 105.
50 Schlegel, PW 105, KA VII, 19. 'Physical' seems here as the opposite of 'political'. For instance: 'political constitution' vs. 'physical constitution'. Schlegel writes: 'In despotism there can be, properly speaking, not a political but only a *physical* constitution', PW 105.
51 Schlegel, PW 105, KA VII, 19. A stimulating discussion of the analogies between Kant's and Fichte's views on representation and those of Émmanuel-Joseph Sieyès is presented by Isaac Nakhimovsky: *The Closed Commercial State. Perpetual Peace and Commercial Society from Rousseau to Fichte*. Princeton: Princeton University Press 2011, 22–61, doi: 10.1515/9781400838752. The connections between Schlegel and Sieyès might be an interesting topic, although Schlegel did not refer explicitly to Sieyès. According to Alain Ruiz, 'Neues über Kant und Sieyès. Ein unbekannter Brief des Philosophen an Anton Ludwig Théremin (März 1796)', *Kant-Studien* 68, no. 4 (1977): 446–453, such a connection might have been incriminating, at least in Prussia 1796. Nevertheless, we know that Schlegel read *Le Moniteur*, and thus had the chance to read Sieyès, KA XXIII, 86; cf. Behler, *Unendliche Perfektibilität. Europäische Romantik und Französische Revolution*, 266–272.
52 Schlegel, PW 105f.; KA VII, 19f.
53 Schlegel, KA VII, 21; PW 108. Marquis de Condorcet, Thomas Paine, and Abbé Sieyès initiated a debate concerning forms of government able to secure a free republic. These positions and their constitutional, social, and economic aspects are discussed in Ruth Scurr, 'Unfreedom and the Republican Tradition in the French Revolution', in *To be Unfree: Republicanism and Unfreedom in History, Literature, and Philosophy*, eds. Christian Dahl and Tue Andersen Nexø (Bielefeld: Transcript Verlag, 2014), 93–115, doi: 10.14361/transcript.9783839421741.93.

Schlegel on Universal Republicanism and the Question of Peace

The analysis presented by Schlegel has so far concerned republicanism in relation to a particular state and people. However, he considered this analysis to be only partial. The political imperative demands a *universal* republicanism based on four points: 1) 'Polizierung aller Nationen' [all nations should be politicized].[54] Presumably, Schlegel here refers to the process of building political communities in a strong sense, i.e., constitutional states. 2) All politicized nations should be republics. 3) All republics should form a brotherhood. 4) Every individual state should be autonomous, and all states should mutually have *isonomía* (i.e. equal rights).[55]

Schlegel's main objection to Kant's definitive articles is that as long as some states remain despotic and some nations are not politicized, the causes of war will subsist. Even imperfect republics will be a threat to peace. Only a universal and perfect republicanism would be a definitive article of peace. According to Schlegel, these, i.e., perfect republicanism and perpetual peace, would be synonymous or coextensive concepts. However, in the meantime, the Kantian definitive articles should only be conceived of as preliminary articles.[56] This brings Schlegel to another very interesting point. Kant holds two trumps to show that the hope that the vision of perpetual peace can become reality in the long run is not in vain. Firstly, he assumes that *nature* will force men to act decently and in cooperation in spite of their individual concerns and egoism. Secondly, the idea of peace is a demand of *reason* – it is what should be the answer if someone asks 'what is right'? It is possible to realize. Thus, it is a duty.

Schlegel, however, found these noble thoughts far-fetched. Kant's reference to the teleology of nature does not matter. What must be considered are *'the laws of political history* and *the principles of political formation'*.[57] Quoting Kant,

---

54 Beiser translates: 'Politicization of all nations' (Schlegel, PW 108).
55 Schlegel, KA VII, 22; PW 108.
56 Schlegel, KA VII, 22f.; PW 109.
57 Schlegel, KA VII, 23. Beiser translates *Bildung* as 'culture' (PW 109). It is, indeed very difficult to identify, what Schlegel meant by 'politische Bildung', although he often underlines differences between ancient political formation (in Attica) and modern political formation. In his anonymously written critique of Condorcet's *Esquisse d'un tableau historique des progrès de l'esprit humain* (1795) (KA VII, 3–10), Schlegel distinguishes between 'sittliche Bildung', 'intellektuelle Bildung', and 'politische Bildung', all being parts of 'der gesamten menschlichen Bildung'. As such, the term *political formation* can refer to Condorcet, and thus indirectly to the huge discussion in revolutionary France concerning educational reforms able to give the masses equal opportunities to show their talent and secure the talented paths to merit via higher education. Condorcet, before his death, was an influential participant in this discussion. Cf. Wilhelm Sjöstrand, *Freedom and Equality as Fundamental Educational Principles in Western Democracy. From John Locke to Edmund Burke* (Stockholm: Föreningen för svensk undervisningshistoria, 1973), 221–289.

Schlegel claims that these are 'the only basis from which we can show "that eternal peace is no empty idea but a task which, as solutions are gradually found, constantly draws near to fulfilment"'.⁵⁸ Now, the history of mankind deals with empirical causes. Thus, Schlegel rejects Kant's quasi-religious denial of human virtue as a necessary condition for civil society, a denial contained in Kant's reference to the realization of a rule of law possible 'even in a nation of devils'.⁵⁹ According to Schlegel, we should not consider the imperfect constitution a problem belonging to 'political art', i.e. the art of politics. Instead, we should consider it a phenomenon belonging to political experience. Precisely the 'theory of political history', and the principles of political formation can *teach* us about the relation between reason and experience in political issues.⁶⁰ Schlegel objects that what Kant understands as political is neither political science nor political art [*raison d'état?*], but rather political 'Pfuscherei' [bungling] affiliated to *despotic* competences.⁶¹

In the last part of his essay, Schlegel deals with the right to insurrection, ardently denied by Kant. Probably also in opposition to Kant's article on *Theory and Praxis* from 1793,⁶² but with obvious reference to *Zum ewigen Frieden*,⁶³ Schlegel argues for the right to insurrection, not as part of any advanced constitution, but as legitimately just in cases where the constitution has been annihilated.⁶⁴ I am not entirely convinced that Schlegel pushes the Kantian project in *Toward Perpetual Peace* in a better direction than Kant did himself. I am afraid that Schlegel overlooked what is perhaps the most amazing innovation in Kant's text, namely the role of publicity in legitimizing actions that can only be carried out through public prescription, in opposition to covert or surreptitious

---

58 Schlegel, PW 109, KA VII, 23.
59 Kant, *Ak.* VIII, 366.
60 I.e., a correct philosophy of political history, if we follow Schlegel's Condorcet critique, cf. Schlegel, KA VII, 4–7. This demands a person: 'der bei unverrücktem Streben, den allgemeinen Gesichtspunkt im Einzelnen zeigen und aus dem Einzelnen den allgemeinen Gesichtspunkt hervorgehen zu lassen, dennoch die Tatsachen nicht verfälscht und verstümmelt, sondern rein und vollständig faßt, sich die scheinbaren Widersprüche nicht verschweigt, sondern die rohe Masse unermüdet so lange durcharbeitet, bis er Licht, Übereinstimmung, Zusammenhang und Ordnung findet ...' ['who, by his adamant efforts to demonstrate the universal point of view in the particular and to move from the particular to the universal point of view, does not tamper with and distort the facts, but rather grasps them in a pure and complete way, does not conceal the apparent contradictions, but relentlessly works through the raw material, until he finds light, consistency, coherence, and order...'.] Schlegel, KA VII, 6f.
61 Schlegel, KA VII, 24; PW 111.
62 Kant, *Ak.* VIII, 299.
63 Kant, *Ak.* VIII, 382.
64 'die Insurrection aber kann nur dann rechtsmäßig sein, wenn die Konstitution vernichtet worden ist' [Insurrection can be legitimate only when the constitution has been already destroyed] Schlegel, KA VII 24f.; PW 111f. Cf. Kant, *Ak.* VIII, 382f.

actions.[65] On the other hand, the demand for public communication somehow recognized by Kant, but limited to rational argumentation, clearly found a broader understanding in the work of the young Friedrich Schlegel. Schlegel, well versed as he was in ancient history and literature, understood the political importance of 'Gespräch' [dialogue]; he understood the importance of *Bildung* and that *Bildung* is not only a demand for self-realization, but for the realization of democracy. However, as pointed out by Beiser: 'When it comes to concrete suggestions about how to educate humanity, about what specific institutional arrangements are to be made, the romantics fall silent'.[66] As we know, the republican position was a brief interlude in Schlegel's life. His journey to France in 1802 confronted him with a political reality that pushed him in a nationalist direction.

[I wish to thank Simon Rolls, Aarhus University, DPU, for language-revision]

---

65 Kant, *Ak.* VIII, 384–386. Cf. Huggler, 'Cosmopolitanism and Peace in Kant's Essay on Perpetual Peace', 138f.
66 Frederick C. Beiser, 'A Romantic Education. The concept of *Bildung* in early German romanticism', in *Philosophers on Education. Historical Perspectives*, ed. Amélie Oksenberg Rorty (London: Routledge, 2004), 297, doi: 10.4324/9780203981610.

Louis Marvick (University of Nevada, Reno) /
Andrew Kent-Marvick (Southern Utah University)

Representing the Vortex: Delacroix's Critique of Poe's Sublime

Abstract
When Eugène Delacroix read Edgar Allan Poe's short story 'A Descent into the Maelstrom' in French translation, he found it tasteless and tedious. In a larger context, his objection seems aimed beyond Poe at the Burkean and Kantian qualities of the sublime exemplified in the story and implies his preference for a restrained and classical standard of sublimity. It also implies his dissatisfaction with the extension in time required for literature to work its effects, as opposed to the singleness and instantaneity of the impression made by painting. The traditional view of Delacroix's development from romantic beginnings to the tame neo-classicism of his final years is reassessed in light of the literary devices that Poe used to heighten the sublime terror of his maelstrom. In the sketches and final versions of paintings executed over a period of thirty-five years, Delacroix is shown to have adopted the painterly equivalents of Poe's hyperbole and litotes as means of evoking the sublimity of the vortex. His attitude towards the wild, romantic sublime was conflicted, and remained unresolved throughout his career.

Keywords
Sublime, Poe, Delacroix, Baudelaire, vortex

The vortex is both the organizing principle of several of Eugène Delacroix's paintings and the subject of Edgar Allan Poe's short story, 'A Descent into the Maelström'. Delacroix did not like Poe's story, and the reasons he gave for his dislike invite critical reflection on a number of points. These include the differences between painting and literature as media suitable for achieving the sublime; the distinct aesthetic traditions that conditioned Poe's and Delacroix's conceptions of sublimity; and the specific literary and painterly means that the two artists employed in striving to give form to those conceptions.

I. Narrative and Lyric Principles in Delacroix's *Journal*

The characteristics that distinguish narrative writing from painting also distinguish it from lyric writing. Narrative takes shape through a temporal series of events requiring attention to the outward circumstances of action. Painting, like lyric writing, can unite the elements of which it is composed in a single vision, a temporal *échappatoire* [loop-hole]. The diachronic and synchronic aspects of the forms are felt in the experiences of reading and viewing: One needs time to read a novel, but one apprehends the whole of a painting, or takes the full dose of a lyric poem, in a single moment. The artist's mind which is the subject of Eugène Delacroix's *Journal* reflects much on this opposition. Delacroix's comments on Edgar Allan Poe, however, seem to contradict the critique of narrative as a time-bound activity which Michele Hannoosh has assembled from entries scattered over several years.[1] The various strands of the painter's thinking about the nature of the literary product and the act of writing come together in an entry of 23 January 1857:

> Je lis depuis quelques jours une histoire d'Edgar Poe qui est celle des naufragés qui sont pendant cinquante pages dans la position la plus horrible et la plus désespérée: rien n'est plus ennuyeux. On reconnaît là le mauvais goût des étrangers. Les Anglais, les Allemands, tous ces peuples antilatins n'ont pas de littérature parce qu'ils n'ont aucune idée du goût et de la mesure. Ils vous assomment avec la situation la plus intéressante. ... Walter Scott, Cooper ... vous noient dans des détails qui ôtent tout l'intérêt'.

> [For several days I have been reading a story by Edgar Poe (Baudelaire's translation of 'A Descent into the Maelström') about castaways who, *for fifty pages*, are in the most horrible and desperate position: nothing could be more boring. One recognizes there the bad taste of foreigners. The English, the Germans, all those anti-Latin peoples, have no literature because they have no idea of taste and measure. They hit you over the head with the most interesting situation. ... Walter Scott, (James Fenimore) Cooper ... drown you in details which take away all the interest.][2]

It is strange to find Poe, Scott, and Cooper all tarred with the same brush. The strictures on Scott and Cooper are fully consistent with what Delacroix elsewhere complains of in narrative writing, namely its tendency to become 'un art bavard' [a prattling art] in which the author 'se compla[ît] à se parler à lui-même' [is pleased to talk to himself]; its reliance on what Hannoosh calls 'the imperatives of length, extent, and progressive linear order'.[3] But Poe's story, though arguably deficient

---
1 See Michele Hannoosh, *Painting and the Journal of Eugène Delacroix* (Princeton, NJ: Princeton University Press, 1995), 9–11, 26–30.
2 Eugène Delacroix, *Journal de Eugène Delacroix*, ed. Paul Flat and René Piot, 3 vols. (Paris: Plon, 1893), 3:233 (italics added). Unless otherwise noted, all translations are our own.
3 Hannoosh, *Painting and the Journal of Eugène Delacroix*, 44. Delacroix quoted in E. A. Piron, *Eugène Delacroix. Sa Vie et ses œuvres* (Paris: Jules Claye, 1865), 408.

with respect 'du goût et de la mesure' [to taste and measure], can hardly be said to be too long. It runs to just twenty-three pages in Baudelaire's 1856 edition, not 'fifty', as Delacroix (with that taste for 'enormous hyperbole' that Baudelaire elsewhere remarked in him) would have it.[4] In its brevity and concentration it exemplifies the first requirement of lyric poetry mentioned in Poe's 'The Philosophy of Composition': it is not 'too long to be read at one sitting'.[5] Delacroix's admission that he has been reading the story 'pendant quelques jours' [for several days], therefore, points to a reluctance to fall in with Poe's purposes. One would not expect the *longueurs* of Scott and Cooper to be found in this work which 'intensely excites ... the soul' by achieving a rigorous 'unity of impression'.[6] So, while there is no doubt that Delacroix finds the story boring, his remark does not make clear *why* he finds it so. The beginnings of an explanation can be found in an earlier comment on Poe in the *Journal* (6 June 1856):

> En rentrant, continué ma lecture d'Edgard Poë [*sic*]. Cette lecture réveille en moi ce sens du mystérieux qui me préoccupait autrefois dans ma peinture. ... Mais l'espèce de décousu et l'incompréhensible qui se mêle à ses conceptions ne va pas à mon esprit.... Il y a de la monotonie dans la fable de toutes ses histoires.
>
> [When I got home, continued my reading of Edgard Poë [*sic*]. This reading awakens in me that sense of the mysterious which used to preoccupy me in my painting.... But the *loosely knit and incomprehensible* quality that mingles with his ideas doesn't suit my mind.... There is something monotonous in the telling of all his stories.][7]

The word 'décousu' [unraveled; loosely knit; coming apart at the seams] belongs to a metaphorical system that appears whenever Delacroix reflects on the nature of writing and composition. The monotony of long narratives arises from the reader's sense that their effect cannot be 'grasped in one sitting'; his attention grows thinner, and finally breaks, as it attempts to follow the narrative 'thread' stretching forward in time.[8] The reader tires of repeating 'le travail qu'il a fallu à l'auteur pour *suivre le fil* de son idée' [the trouble it cost the author to *follow the thread* of his idea].[9] Even where Delacroix speaks of 'stitching together' the parts

---

4 Edgar Poe, 'Une Descente dans le Maelstrom', *Histoires extraordinaires*', trans. Charles Baudelaire (Paris: Michel Lévy, 1856), 221–244. Subsequent citations from Baudelaire's translation refer to a standard modern edition, Edgar Allan Poe, *Prose*, trans. Charles Baudelaire, ed. Y.-G. Le Dantec (Paris: Gallimard, 'Bibliothèque de la Pléiade', 1951), 193–211. The remark on Delacroix's taste for hyperbole is in Charles Baudelaire, 'L'Œuvre et la vie de Delacroix', *Œuvres complètes*', 2 vols., ed. Claude Pichois (Paris: Gallimard, 'Bibliothèque de la Pléiade', 1976), 2:764.
5 Edgar Allan Poe, 'The Philosophy of Composition', *Essays and Reviews*, ed. G. R. Thompson (New York: The Library of America, 1984), 15.
6 Ibid., 15.
7 Delacroix, *Journal*, 3:150–51 (italics added).
8 Hannoosh, *Painting*, 65, 94.
9 Delacroix, *Journal*, 1:439 (italics added).

of a composition into a satisfactory whole, he implicitly acknowledges the inevitable presence of this 'thread'.[10] His *Dictionnaire des beaux-arts* was to consist of 'pensées détachées' [detached thoughts] collected, unbound, in a box; the entries would not be fixed in temporal sequence but could be read singly, or in any combination.[11] (In this, the *Dictionnaire* would have resembled Baudelaire's *Spleen de Paris*, of which the poet remarked that its contents were not connected by 'le fil interminable d'une intrigue superflue' [the tedious thread of an unnecessary plot].)[12] Yet the metaphor that informs this strategy for overcoming the tyranny of time over literary form returns to defeat it. The shortest book is still 'trop long' [too long].[13] Even the single page consists of words strung together (or of ideas extruded through a narrow aperture), and can therefore never give the satisfaction of a composition in the pictorial sense.[14] Writing is still 'a matter of stitching thoughts to other thoughts'.[15] Although each 'detached thought' of the *Dictionnaire* was conceived as 'a discreet unit like an image', the adjective 'détachée' betrays its connection to a still unassembled whole.[16] Each small, focused entry would be like a photograph taking its place among other 'parties détachées d'un tout' [parts detached from a whole], or like one of the 'parties du corps humain' [parts of the human body] that apprentices are obliged to 'copi[er] sans fin… sans s'élever jusqu'à la composition' [copy endlessly… without rising to the level of composition].[17]

In his remarks on the paintings whose subjects Delacroix derived from literary sources, Baudelaire suggests a way of understanding how the painter sought to collapse into a single moment the succession of events whose interest grew fainter in the time it took to read about them. He did this, Baudelaire says, by reducing 'le drame' [drama] to 'le geste' [gesture]: 'En fait de gestes sublimes, Delacroix n'a de rivaux' [As regards sublime gestures, Delacroix has no rivals].[18] His 'essentially literary' sensibility gives the essence of its written sources by 'the dramatic gesticulation of his figures 'What we admire above all in him [is] the

---

10 '[E]n écrivant… il ne s'agi[t] que de coudre des pensées à d'autres pensées' [(W)riting […] is only a matter of stitching thoughts to other thoughts]. Delacroix, *Journal*, 2:14.
11 Delacroix adopted this phrase from Diderot and 'frequently alluded to his critical ideal as "pensées détachées"' (Hannoosh, *Painting*, 102).
12 Charles Baudelaire, dedicatory letter of *Le Spleen de Paris* in *Œuvres complètes*, 1:275.
13 Delacroix (quoting Voltaire), *Journal*, 3:204.
14 'Pour formuler des idées… il faut… les passer par une embouchure un peu rétrécie qui les moule en les mettant au jour' [To formulate ideas… one must… put them through a rather narrow opening which molds them as it brings them forth]. Letter to Balzac quoted and translated in Hannoosh, *Painting*, 28.
15 Delacroix, *Journal*, 2:14.
16 Hannoosh, *Painting*, 65.
17 Delacroix, *Journal*, 3:267, followed by Eugène Delacroix, 'L'Enseignement du dessin', *Ecrits sur l'art*, ed. François-Marie Deyrolle and Christophe Denissel (Paris: Séguier, 1988), 52.
18 Baudelaire, *Salon de 1846*, *Œuvres complètes*, 2:441.

suddenness of the gesture', like that found in writers 'whose sentence resembles a gesture'.[19] Baudelaire seems to imply that the striking gesture sums up the action that precedes it and follows it in the drama, and marks the moment when (as Elizabeth Abel has said) 'the outcome could go either way'.[20] The point might be related to the classical principle of unity of action, or to the love of concentration expressed, some years later, in Mallarmé's dictum, 'Il faut toujours couper le commencement et la fin de ce qu'on écrit. Pas d'introduction, pas de finale' [One must always cut the beginning and end of what one writes. No introduction, no finale].[21] But, as regards the difference between narrative and painting, another application is more pertinent. Insofar as the scenes of the drama succeed one another in time, they may be said to follow a narrative order; but 'un tableau… consiste en une *série de tableaux superposés*, chaque nouvelle couche donnant au rêve plus de réalité et le faisant monter d'un degré vers la perfection' [a painting… consists of a *series of superimposed paintings*, each new layer giving more reality to the dream and causing it to rise by a degree toward perfection].[22] The moments of the narrative are thus presented, not in series, but in depth, with those preceding the climax helping to shape the final composition; rising to its surface as if in *pentimento*. The gesture contributes vitally to this effect, which has been described as 'a sense of continuous movement… as though the object were not wholly fixed in space'.[23] A painting by Delacroix is thus the expansion *within a single moment* of an action which narrative must parcel out in successive episodes, and drama in successive scenes.[24]

A proof of this can be found in the program note that Delacroix wrote for his painting, 'Apollo Vanquishing the Python' (1851). The actions antecedent to the moment depicted in the finished composition are all mentioned in the present perfect tense: 'Le dieu… *a déjà lancé* une partie de ses traits…. *Déjà percé* par les flèches… le monstre sanglant se tord… Les dieux *se sont indignés*… Ils *se sont armés* comme Apollon' [The god… *has already hurled* some of his bolts…

---

19 '[I]l est essentiellement littéraire…. la dramatique gesticulation de ses figures'. Baudelaire, *Exposition universelle (1855)*, *Œuvres complètes*, 2:596. '[C]e que nous admirons surtout en lui, [c'est] la soudaineté dans le geste….' Delacroix favored 'les écrivains… dont la phrase ressemble à un geste'. Baudelaire, 'L'Œuvre et la vie de Delacroix', *Œuvres complètes*, 2:754-55.
20 Elizabeth Abel, 'Redefining the Sister Arts: Baudelaire's Response to the Art of Delacroix', *Critical Inquiry* 6.3 (1980), 363-84.
21 Stéphane Mallarmé, *Correspondance*, 3 vols., ed. Henri Mondor and Jean-Pierre Richard (Paris: Gallimard, 1959-1969), 1:117.
22 Baudelaire, 'L'Œuvre et la vie de Delacroix', 2:749 (italics added).
23 Lee Johnson, *Delacroix* (London: Weidenfeld and Nicolson, 1963), 79.
24 Cf. Delacroix, *Journal*, 2:14: 'Vous voyez votre tableau d'un coup d'œil; dans votre manuscrit, vous ne voyez pas même la page entière, c'est-à-dire, vous ne pouvez pas l'embrasser tout entière par l'esprit [You see a painting with a glance; in your manuscript you do not even see the whole page, that is, you cannot embrace it completely with your mind].

Already pierced by the arrows... the bleeding monster writhes... The gods *have become* angry... They *have armed* themselves like Apollo].[25] The terminative aspect of these verbs binds them to the present moment from which they are viewed, and which, together, they have defined.

Taken together, these observations may complicate our perplexity, for in many of them Delacroix agrees with Poe. In 'The Philosophy of Composition' Poe writes about the 'pivot' of a narrative action, the importance of the *dénouement*, the degree of suggestion that a single image can be made to carry, and the 'circumscription of space' that has 'the force of a frame to a picture'.[26] This close resemblance makes Delacroix's dislike of 'A Descent into the Maelström' puzzling. On the other hand, his remarks about Poe's lack of 'measure' and 'taste' are consistent with his insistence on the effect of variety-in-unity which the compression of several narrative events into a single image achieves. Poe's story takes place entirely on the vertical axis, beginning at the top of a mountain and descending to the bottom of the whirlpool. There is in it no varied sequence of incidents to be compressed; not 'too many' things, but 'too much' of a single thing.

II. Taming the Sublime

Delacroix's claim that Poe's failure of taste in 'A Descent into the Maelström' is typical of 'ces peuples antilatins [qui] n'ont aucune idée du goût et de la mesure' [those anti-Latin peoples (who) have no idea of taste and measure] seems especially significant in the context of Baudelaire's reference to the painter's mastery of the 'geste sublime' [sublime gesture].[27] For it is precisely as an episode in the history of disagreement over the nature of the sublime that Delacroix's disparagement of Poe makes sense. One may distinguish two fundamentally opposed traditions. In France, the sublime was understood primarily as the effect of rhetoric first described in *Peri hypsous*, a second-century Greek treatise incorrectly attributed to Longinus and translated by Boileau in 1688 as the *Traité du sublime*. In the opening verses of Genesis, as in the most pitched moments of seventeenth-century French tragedy, 'great thoughts' are conveyed with an austere simplicity and economy of language. Longinus illustrates the effect by quoting the lines, 'God said, "Let there be light", and there was light'; but French readers since Boileau were more likely to think of scenes from Racine or

---

25 The passage is quoted in full in Baudelaire, 'L'Œuvre et la vie de Delacroix', 2:755–56 (italics added).
26 Poe, 'The Philosophy of Composition', 21.
27 Baudelaire, *Salon de 1846*, *Œuvres complètes*, 2:441; see note 18 above.

Corneille in which the pressure of an archetypal human dilemma provokes a supremely concentrated utterance.[28] In the cultural context which surrounded Baudelaire's characterization of Delacroix's 'sublime gesture', then, the sublime was closely associated with the motives, scale and description of *human* action.[29]

But the 'anti-Latin peoples' whose lack of 'measure' Delacroix deplored were conscious of a different meaning. The sublime tradition which Edgar Allan Poe had come to know in the pages of *Blackwood's Magazine* was directly related to the English Gothic Revival and, through it, to German *Schauerromantik*. Instead of to the neo-classical Longinus of Boileau's translation, it looked to Edmund Burke's and Immanuel Kant's treatises on the sublime for definition and direction. The two texts are complementary and together constitute a sort of theoretical manifesto for Poe's experiment in 'A Descent into the Maelström'.[30] Burke emphasizes the sensational means of producing feelings of 'awe' and 'terror' in which the subject takes pleasure by realizing that the cause of those feelings is a 'fiction'.[31] He is much concerned with the phenomena of nature to be imitated and dwells upon those characterized by the presence of an extreme contrast between light and darkness, or height and depth. Kant's explanation of the pleasure to be found in the experience of overpowering effects of nature resembles Burke's in referring that experience to the faculty of aesthetic judgment: We take pleasure in 'might [i.e., power] that has no dominion over us' – in storms and avalanches represented in painting or literature, for example, or otherwise contemplated from a safe remove – because that 'might' gives us 'an idea of fearfulness' without making us 'afraid *of* it'.[32] In contrast to beauty, which is always apprehended in the *form* of an object, the sublime involves a judgment of the 'absolutely' great.[33] Spectacles of nature which, by virtue of their number or power (the so-called 'mathematical' and 'dynamical' versions of sublimity) force us to recognize the inadequacy of our senses and imagination, can only be addressed by reason, 'a

---

28 See Jules Brody, *Boileau and Longinus* (Geneva: Droz, 1958), 91: 'To the example of the *Fiat lux* [in Genesis] he [Boileau] added that of the famous "*Qu'il mourût*" [*He should have died*] in Corneille's *Horace*'. Boileau observes that 'c'est la simplicité même de ce mot qui en fait la grandeur' [it is the very simplicity of this utterance that makes it great]. Baudelaire noted Delacroix's mastery of 'la vérité emphatique du geste dans les grandes circonstances de la vie' [the emphatic truth of the gesture in the great moments of life]. *Exposition universelle (1855)*, *Œuvres complètes*, 2:592.
29 Baudelaire points out how Delacroix liked to disconcert the proponents of romanticism by praising the virtues of classical restraint; see 'L'Œuvre et la vie de Delacroix', 2:754.
30 Edmund Burke, *A Philosophical Enquiry into the Origin of Our Ideas on the Sublime and Beautiful* [1757], *The Works of the Right Honorable Edmund Burke*, 12 vols. (London: Nimmo, 1887), 2:67–262. Immanuel Kant, 'Analytic of the Sublime', *Critique of Judgement* [1764], trans. J. H. Bernard (London: Macmillan, 1914), 101–131.
31 Burke, *A Philosophical Inquiry*, 241, 120.
32 Kant, 'Analytic', 123–24.
33 Ibid., 120.

faculty of the mind surpassing every standard of sense'.[34] This failure of our imagination and resort to reason pleases us by demonstrating our connection, through reason, with the absolute.

It is striking how systematically, in 'A Descent into the Maelström', Poe applies the principles of Kant and Burke, as if his object were to demonstrate their validity as a strategy for achieving the sublime. Yet, though striking, it is not surprising in one who claimed always to 'commenc[e] with the consideration of an *effect*', and then, by 'cautious selections and rejections', by 'painful erasures and interpolations', undertook to achieve it in the most efficient manner.[35] Burke's emphasis on 'extreme contrast' and 'intense light or darkness' is reflected on every page of Poe's story. The series of juxtaposed extremes begin on the homeliest level with the subject of the descent, the 'old man', explaining to the framing narrator that in just 'six hours of deadly terror' his hair had changed 'from a jetty black to white'.[36] This transformation is immediately established as an effect of conditions in the old man's environment that mirror it: the 'inky' hue of the water, the 'horridly black' cliffs are emphasized by the 'white' surf against them.[37] Extremes of light and dark, of black and white, are presented on the most staggering scale before returning, at the very end of the story, to the same marker of their human reflection: 'My hair, which had been raven black the day before, was as white as you see it now'.[38] In between, the sea, 'black as pitch', has been illuminated by the 'full moon... blaz[ing] forth'; the blackness of the 'abyss' has been emphasized by the white 'belt of surf... surround[ing] the whirl'; the walls of the vortex look like 'ebony' in 'the radiance... of the full moon'.[39] The starkness of this contrast is consistent with Burke's principle that 'the power of black as black, or of white as white, [is never] so strong as when each stands uniform and distinguished'; while its suddenness, as seen in the blenching of the old man's hair, fulfills Burke's requirement of 'a quick transition... from darkness to light'.[40]

---

34 Ibid., 110.
35 Poe, 'The Philosophy of Composition', 13-14.
36 Edgar Allan Poe, 'A Descent into the Maelström' (1841), *Poetry and Tales*, ed. Patrick F. Quinn (New York: The Library of America, 1984), 432.
37 Ibid., 433.
38 Ibid., 448.
39 Ibid., 441, 442, 444.
40 Burke, *A Philosophical Enquiry*, 156, 207. Daniel Tobias Seger, 'Stürze in den Malstrom: Edgar Allan Poes "A Descent into the Maelström" im Horizont von Kants "Analytik des Erhabenen" ', *Literaturwissenschaftliches Jahrbuch*, 42 (2001), 225-43, argues that the striking detail of the old man's hair turning white, like other aspects of the story, ignores 'the law of probability', and forces the reader to consign Poe's tale to Todorov's realm of the marvelous, rather than to the fantastic (231). To be valid, this argument would require readers of the story *at the time of its original publication* (1841) to have perceived a lack of verisimilitude in such details.

Cooperating with the extremes of light and dark are those of height and depth, likewise conflated in such a way as to defy the rule of nature and boggle the reader's mind. The rule is established at the beginning of the story, where the vertical and horizontal dimensions are presented on a scale that fills, without quite exceeding, the imagination: from 'the summit of the loftiest crag' the old man and his companion peer down 'a sheer unobstructed precipice of black shining rock' to 'the vast bed of the waters'.[41] Having established the framework of nature in its uttermost extension, the story strains at it and breaks it apart by recounting the unnatural 'descent' below sea level. Normal *up* and *down* are confounded by the irruption of the monstrous whirlpool, a phenomenon of nature so singular and outsize that it threatens to cancel the axes by which the old man and the reader have just oriented themselves. Thus 'the seas, which at first... lay flat... got up into absolute mountains'; 'the world of ocean... arose... like a huge writhing wall between us and the horizon'; 'the general bed of the ocean... now towered above us, a high, black, mountainous ridge'.[42]

The description repeatedly implies that the maelstrom exists in defiance of nature, as if to convince the reader that her imagination cannot possibly accommodate it. Thus the skiff, in the course of its descent, is said to lie 'upon an even keel' yet 'upon [its] beam-ends', the water itself having 'sloped [to] an angle of more than forty-five degrees'.[43] The extremes of light and dark and of height and depth are brought together at last in a single appalling image that obliterates their connection with the world of natural forms and, thus, their utility for reference. Having asserted as a matter of putative fact that 'in the centre of the channel of the maelstrom is an abyss penetrating the globe', the old man reports that 'the rays of the moon seemed to search the very bottom of the profound gulf'.[44] Thus the highest and brightest object in the night sky is turned into a vehicle for the utmost hyperbole of darkness and depth, and the reader is challenged to imagine the act of searching the bottom of an abyss that has been said to be bottomless.

Longinus repeatedly mentions hyperbole among the figures of rhetoric that tend to excite a sense of the sublime.[45] The precept is not lost on Poe, who variously compares the noise of the whirlpool to the mightiest phenomena of nature only to deny that the comparison is adequate. Thus 'a vast herd of buf-

---

41 Poe, 'A Descent', 432, 434. This gambit is consistent with Burke's remark that 'height is less grand than depth... we are more struck at looking down from a precipice, than looking up at an object of equal height'. Burke, *A Philosophical Enquiry*, 147.
42 Poe, 'A Descent', 441, 442, 443.
43 Ibid., 445.
44 Ibid., 437, 445.
45 Longinus, *On the Sublime, Classical Literary Criticism*, trans. T. S. Dorsch (Harmondsworth: Penguin, 1965), 97–158.

faloes', 'the mighty cataract of Niagara', 'the loudest and most dreadful cataracts', and the 'howlings and bellowings of whales and of bears' are considered and rejected in turn.[46] As has been suggested elsewhere, hyperbole is an effective approach to the sublime because it is open-ended: in a single trope, the most stupendous comparison is both offered and dismissed, leaving the reader with the pleasing sense that her imagination is free to fly beyond it (the Greek word means 'beyond the target').[47] In several places, a related figure also recommended by Longinus is used, namely *ploce* (in Latin manuals *praeteritio*; saying something while claiming not to say it). The vivid description of the storm is prefaced by assurances that 'it is folly to attempt describing [it]'; that the description itself is 'exceedingly feeble' and 'cannot impart the faintest conception' of the reality.[48] As with hyperbole, the aim is to offer an image of unsurpassable size and power while leaving open the possibility of something still greater – a reality beyond the *ne plus ultra* of the imagination.

Even more significant for our argument than either of these figures, however, is the figure of *litotes*, or understatement for the purpose of exaggeration; a comparison in which the tenor is magnified by a vehicle that seems to diminish it. In 'A Descent into the Maelström' Poe uses litotes in a measured, step-like way, suggesting that he was familiar with the notion of the 'mathematical' sublime advanced in Kant's *Analytic*.[49] The trope occurs in the story's opening paragraphs. So deeply was the old man affected by his experience of the maelstrom, he says, that merely to look down from the summit of the 'little cliff' which he and the narrator have ascended makes him feel 'giddy'.[50] Yet this 'little cliff' is really Mount Helseggen, towering 'some fifteen or sixteen hundred feet' above the 'world of crags' below; crags which are themselves the summits of mountains that rise to an unknown height above sea level.[51] The reader must infer that, in the same degree that Mount Helseggen is greater than a 'little cliff', the maelstrom is greater than Mount Helseggen. But this degree of difference is made *unimaginable* by the stupendous hyperbole of size applied to the mountain. Even in relative calm, without the maelstrom being present, 'the fury of the winds' is such as to make the narrator think that 'the very foundations of the mountains were in danger'.[52] The reader is asked to imagine a power greater – and greater in a

---

46 Ibid., 434, 435, 436.
47 See Louis Marvick, *Mallarmé and the Sublime* (New York: State University of New York Press, 1986), 57–61.
48 Poe, 'A Descent', 440, 435.
49 Baudelaire repeatedly stresses Poe's supposed expertise in mathematics in the preface to his 1856 translation ('Edgar Poe, sa Vie et ses Œuvres', *Prose*, 1042–59).
50 Poe, 'A Descent', 432.
51 Ibid., 432.
52 Ibid., 433.

mathematically estimable degree – than that required to shake the foundations of natural objects so great that the narrator can only '*reason [him]self* into sufficient courage... to look' at them.⁵³ This resort to reason at the point at which the imagination collapses is precisely the mental operation described in Kant's *Analytic of the Sublime*.

Step-like comparisons do not always fall under the heading of litotes, even where they seem to. For example, the narrator asserts that 'the largest ships of the line' could no more resist the power of the maelstrom than 'a feather the hurricane'.⁵⁴ In the same degree that a ship of the line is greater than a feather (we must understand), the maelstrom is greater than a hurricane. So far, so good. But when the narrator adds that 'Our boat was the lightest feather of a thing', we are not meant to infer (as litotes would have us do) that the boat was really as great as a ship of the line.⁵⁵ On the contrary, the aim is clearly to emphasize the lightness and fragility of the boat and, at the same time, the incommensurable power and greatness of the maelstrom.

Here and elsewhere, the function of the comparison seems to be to keep the small end of the scale of smallness and greatness present to the reader's mind. However great it is said to be, the maelstrom must still retain some connection with the terms of human experience. If it did not, the necessary act of imaginative failure and intellectual transcendence could not take place. Thus it is not only 'the very foundations of the mountains [that] were in danger', not only 'The mountain [that] trembled to its very base', but also 'the very stones of the houses' and the person of the narrator himself, which 'shook from head to foot' as if with 'the most violent fit of the ague'.⁵⁶ Similarly, the sequence of natural phenomena evoked to give an idea of the noise that issues from the bottom of the whirlpool culminates in a return to the level of sentient creatures: it is a 'yell', 'an appalling voice, half shriek, half roar'.⁵⁷ At the uttermost extreme of inhuman magnitude, the narrator discovers a terrifying kinship with flesh and blood.⁵⁸

Poe's attention to the small and ordinary as a counterpoise to the gigantic and appalling informs the story at every level. One finds it not only in details (such as the mention of the 'brig in the remote offing' that establishes scale before the onset of the storm, or the assertion that 'no particle' of spray 'slipped into the

---

53 Ibid., 433; italics added.
54 Ibid., 437.
55 Ibid., 440.
56 Ibid., 433, 435, 436, 441.
57 Ibid., 445, 435.
58 Burke mentions that 'the angry tones of wild beasts are... capable of causing a great and awful sensation' (*A Philosophical Enquiry*, 162). Poe uses the figure of praeteritio in connection with this metaphor, as well. Having described the noise with great vividness, the narrator protests that he 'dare not attempt to describe it' (445). After surviving the ordeal, he is left 'speechless from the memory of its horror' (448).

mouth of the terrific funnel' which has grown to 'more than a mile in diameter'), but in the repeated alternation of a passage of highly wrought description with one of pedestrian calculation.[59] These changes of tone are so marked as to divide the story into three distinct sections, each repeating (but each time with greater intensity) much the same leap from the mundane to the inconceivable. Following the first accretion of hyperbole, the narrator recollects 'the ordinary account' of one 'Jonas Ramus'; this begins with a sober measurement in fathoms and minute geographical orientation before building to a second, even more staggering climax, which in turn is relayed by unexciting information about the old man's daily routine and the draft of his fishing vessel.[60] Here, significantly, numbers become prominent, and the danger of 'miscalculation' is mentioned.[61] Numbers – the means by which reason measures the impressions of the senses – serve to 'ground' the old man during his descent. But with the third and most terrifying climax he is struck by 'the fact of [his] invariable miscalculation' and loses this defense against the fear of imminent death.[62]

The failure of the resort to numbers illustrates the 'unbounded' quality of the sublime feeling described by Burke and Kant, and at the same time helps to explain Poe's choice of literary means. The sublime, Kant says, 'is the name given to what is *absolutely great*'; that is, '*what is great beyond all comparison*'.[63] It follows that the attempt to measure phenomena which give rise to the feeling of the sublime is bound to fail, for 'the computation of the magnitude of phenomena... is always based on comparison'.[64] Any 'measure assumed as a known quantity' will prove incapable of compassing 'that in comparison with which all else is small'; and since 'reason demands [an] absolute totality' which incremental measurements cannot give, the mind is forced to abandon the act of counting and recognize the existence of 'a supersensible faculty within [itself]'.[65] This intuition of infinity – of 'limitlessness' combined with 'totality'; of what 'is absolutely (not merely comparatively) great' – is found in a reflexive turning away

---

59 Poe, 'A Descent', 434, 435. Poe's use of both the sublime and humble styles has a parallel in Edmund Burke, who, as Conor Cruise O'Brien noted, switches from the 'Gothic and pathetic' style familiar from anthologies of purple prose to the 'rational, perspicacious, business-like' style meant to convince skeptical Parliamentarians of the soundness of his proposals. Conor Cruise O'Brien, "Introduction: The Manifesto of a Counter-Revolution" in Edmund Burke, *Reflections on the Revolution in France* (Harmondsworth: Penguin, 1986), 42–43. Cf. Poe, 'The Philosophy of Composition': 'Passion [demands] a *homeliness*' which is 'antagonistic' to the 'pleasurable elevation of the soul'; this element may be 'profitably introduced [to] aid the general effect' (16–17; italics in original).
60 Poe, 'A Descent', 435, 437.
61 Ibid., 438.
62 Ibid., 446.
63 Kant, 'Analytic of the Sublime', 106; italics in original.
64 Ibid., 107.
65 Ibid., 109–10.

from phenomena towards 'our own ideas'.[66] Similarly, Burke (writing in what Kant, some thirty-five years later, would call a 'merely empirical' perspective, namely one in which no distinction between sensible and 'supersensible' powers of judgment is made) characterizes 'the infinite' as 'the idea of a perfect unity... to which nothing may be added': infinity 'causes much of our pleasure...in sublime images...because the imagination is entertained with the promise of something more, and does not acquiesce in the present object of sense'.[67]

Poe's choice of hyperbole, litotes, and praeteritio as the rhetorical means of inducing a sense of the sublime is now readily understandable, for these are all figures of comparison that carry within them a mechanism for rejecting the very idea of comparison. In each, the 'unit of measurement', or vehicle – 'feathers' for ships of the line; 'little cliffs' for mountains – is mentioned only in order to be exceeded (hyperbole), belittled (litotes), or dismissed as inadequate (praeteritio).

For Poe, as for Kant, the sublime is not finally a matter of scenery but of rising through terror and 'outrage on the imagination' to the highest level of human nature, which is a moral level.[68] As Kant puts it, when the mind is driven to 'employ itself upon ideas involving higher finality' it recognizes its ability to conceive 'the idea of a noumenon'; this recognition carries with it a sense of the obligation to demonstrate 'a disposition that is upright and acceptable to God'.[69] Like the moral law embodied in the Categorical Imperative, 'delight in the sublime' must 'be shown to be universally valid' and 'independent of interest'.[70] The key event in 'A Descent into the Maelström' illustrates this principle. At the climax of the second development, the narrator's brother, 'in the agony of his terror', forces the narrator's hands from the ringbolt to which he clings. By this act, Poe links what Kant would call the faculties of moral and aesthetic judgment. 'Sheer fright' drives the brother to prefer his immediate self-interest to the law against fratricide that should determine his conduct. At the same time, it prevents him from achieving the detachment necessary to view the maelstrom as an occasion of the sublime. The narrator, in contrast, is able 'to reflect how magnificent a thing it was to die in such a manner, and how foolish it was in me to think of so paltry a consideration as my own individual life, in view of so wonderful a manifestation of God's power'.[71] His detachment allows him both to 'gaze about' himself with 'admira-

---

66 Ibid., 117.
67 Ibid., 147–49. Burke, *A Philosophical Enquiry*, 148, 154.
68 Kant, 'Analytic', 116.
69 Ibid., 116.
70 Ibid., 105, 134.
71 Poe, 'A Descent', 443–44. Cf. Camille Mauclair, *Le Génie d'Edgar Poe* (Paris, 1925), 123: 'The fisherman is freed from his fear by an almost serene contemplation of the impassive Law which brought the fear about. To understand this Law is to be consoled for falling victim to it'. Quoted in Patrick F. Quinn, *The French Face of Edgar Poe* (Carbondale: Southern Illinois UP, 1954), 60.

tion' and, more practically, to observe that by clinging to a barrel he will not sink. His brother's exemplary failure to rise above his terror, on the other hand, causes him to plunge both literally and metaphysically into the abyss.

III. The Vortex

A better subject for Delacroix's critical reflection than Poe's picture of the whirlpool would be difficult to find, for there is no visual device more iconic in the corpus of romantic painting than the vortex, and none which recurs more persistently (though idiosyncratically, as will be explained) in the œuvre of Delacroix. The paintings considered below reveal an equivocal attitude toward the imposition of restraining forces on the romantic sublime that recalls the inconsistencies identified in Delacroix's writings on the theme; they will allow us to trace nuances in Delacroix's exploration of a romantic sublime (vis-à-vis a classicizing/taming impulse) *over time*, and to appreciate how those nuances parallel the ones already identified in Delacroix's written remarks on the subject. This suite of pictorially similar canvases was executed over a period of many years, and as a result, the mechanisms by which energy was intensified or tempered from picture to picture emerge vividly from them. The choice of this series of Arab conflict scenes is not arbitrary, but serves (a.) to exemplify Delacroix's formal strategies for the expression of a French romantic sublime, and (b.) to document his tendency to re-think – and alternately to intensify and relax – the same theme across decades.

The vortex is implied as early as 1822 in the interlocking planes of *Dante and Virgil in Hell*, the painter's first great public success. A long and well-established critical consensus with respect to Delacroix's formal expression has stressed the artist's efforts to classicize, and so to tame, this motif in a series of late, large-scale works (*The Triumph of Apollo* [1851], *Jason Wrestling with the Angel* [1857–1861] and *Arabs Skirmishing in the Mountains* [1863]), and has inferred from these late efforts a shift in his formal strategies – away from the concentrated and intimate record of a single moment which characterized the early works of the 1820s (such as *Dante and Virgil in Hell* and *The Natchez* [1823]) toward more loosely woven compositions that might accommodate a temporal narrative.[72]

---

[72] It was Baudelaire who first drew attention to the classicizing tendency of Delacroix's brand of the sublime, when he famously declared that 'Delacroix était passionnément amoureux de la passion, et froidement déterminé à chercher les moyens d'exprimer la passion de la manière la plus visible' [Delacroix was passionately in love with passion, and coldly determined to seek the means of expressing passion in the most visible possible manner] ('L'Œuvre et la vie d'Eugène Delacroix', Œuvres complètes, 2:746). Most notably among modern scholars, Walter Friedlaender explored this dualism in *David to Delacroix* (Cambridge, Mass.: Harvard

That shift is perceptible in the space between 1826, when Delacroix painted *The Combat of the Giaour and Hassan* (Figure 1) and 1861, the year of the Art Institute of Chicago's famous *Lion Hunt* (Figure 2), a painting which made explicit Delacroix's abiding respect for the art of the Flemish baroque master Peter Paul Rubens (1577–1640), whose own *Lion Hunt* of 1621 was among a group of paintings that initiated centuries of so-called Orientalist genre. In his expression of contempt for Poe and other 'anti-Latins' of the Anglo-American school, Delacroix cites the want of 'taste' and 'measure' – both terms tied closely to classical principles of design in the visual arts – as grounds for his disdain; in the same sentence he connects the failure to observe these principles with an excess of information, specific detail, and narrative time, the result of which is boredom. His linkage of classical design principles to the *avoidance* of temporality and mimetic precision (in favor of a holistic and generalized, atemporal effect) is the central paradox of Delacroix's art, and one which becomes particularly visible in later works. The classical principles to which Delacroix refers in both early and late journal entries are disguised in the paintings themselves – cloaked, so to speak, in the rich and heavy brocade of Rubensian color and application. By 1861, however, it is clear that Delacroix could fairly be called a natural inheritor of the 'classical' French sensibility originated by Nicolas Poussin (1594–1665) and his younger contemporaries, Laurent de La Hyre and Eustache Le Sueur. Delacroix took up their seventeenth-century French courtly models of compositional integrity within the image (pyramidal, boxed and oval figure arrangements) and attendant regular (three-beat, four-beat and whorling) rhythms and adapted them to his own dramatic subjects and distinctive chromatic and painterly idiom.[73]

Yet Delacroix was equally attracted to the liberal rhythmic motion which Rubens's *Tiger Hunt* of 1616 offered as an alternative to Le Sueur's and de La Hyre's precisely measured classicism, and both his early and late treatments of the theme reflect this potential conflict. In the final hunt scene of 1861 (Figure 2), for example, Delacroix's revisiting of Rubens's theme evolves not from a re-

---

University Press, 1952 [1980]), arguing for example that the *Lion Hunt* series were 'Delacroix's attempt... to clarify certain confusions in composition which he believed present in Rubens' (122). Andrea S. Honore exemplifies recent scholarship on the theme: 'it is... important to acknowledge Delacroix's conception of himself as part of the continuing tradition of great painter-decorators from Michelangelo and Titian to Nicolas Poussin and Charles Le Brun, and to note his acceptance of David among the modern exponents of this tradition' ('A Pastel Study for "The Death of Sardanapalus" by Eugène Delacroix', *Art Institute of Chicago Museum Studies* 2.1 [1995], 9). Stephanie Moira has provided further support for this view, explaining that the artist did not equate classicism with style but instead saw it as a reflection of a 'Homeric spirit' that permitted the inclusion of Rubens, for example, in the classicists' ranks ('Delacroix's Art Theory and His Definition of Classicism', *The Journal of Aesthetic Education* 34.1 [Spring 2000] 61).

73 As an example of the first of these types, see La Hyre's *Thésée et Éthra* (1635–1640), and of the second, Le Sueur's *La Réunion d'amis* (1640).

Fig. 1: Eugène Delacroix, *The Combat of the Giaour and Hassan* [*Le Combat du Giaour et de Hassan*], 1826. Oil on canvas 23 2/5 x 28 4/5 inches (59.6 x 73.4 cm), Art Institute of Chicago

jection of French classicism, but from a new amalgamation with it. The sinuous impasto that travels, in near-riotous thickets of hatched strokes, around the musculature of the fallen horse in the 1861 painting is a clear sign of Delacroix's personal romantic style – yet it evinces self-restraint, not license: despite multiple spirals of flesh and fabric, bristling masses of short, cross-hatched strokes and punctuation marks of saturated cadmium red, the *Lion Hunt* of 1861 in fact shows Delacroix holding himself in check, imposing on Rubens's model the compositional and rhythmic devices of Poussin, and positioning himself at a safe remove from the limits of both his natural inclinations and his hard-won technical facility. Although the well-known position of Delacroix in opposition to Ingres invites the characterization of this tendency as a classicizing one, a fairer description of the later Delacroix is that it seemed to tame a *wilder* sublime through the governing agency of a *French* sublime. One look into the relative chaos of the 1854 oil sketch of the *Lion Hunt* (Figure 3) shows what care, calculation, and attention to decorum, by contrast, were brought to the finished version of this composition in the following year (Figure 4).

Fig. 2: Eugène Delacroix, *The Lion Hunt* [*La Chasse au lion*], 1861. Oil on canvas, 30 x 38 1/2 inches (76.5 x 98.5 cm), Art Institute of Chicago

The study is furious; its scarce-begun contours (for example, the abstraction of black and gold which merely suggests the head of the rearing steed in the top center of the composition) and frenetic brushwork have barely survived in the later treatment. Yet, both the study and the gallery painting date from Delacroix's late years – despite his embrace, as early as 1832, of the virtues of momentum. Color – particularly the interlace of crimson with stains of blue in the gilded whites – here offers an early and characteristic demonstration of the 'vibration' with which the Impressionists would later become so closely linked.[74] Yet color, given direction and form by the Arab's flowing *dishdasha* and cape, is turned to the service of a single, central focal point: the fighters' scimitars and the strokes they portend. A single compositional foil offers balance, but not relief: a horseless third figure at the bottom right forces the picture's propulsive energy back toward the left; that is, back into the fray. As a result of these measures, the collection of figures is seen in unity, bypassing the sequential strategies of temporal narrative.

---

74 Jerome Mellquist identified this link in Delacroix's *Horses Coming out of the Sea,* which, he argued, proved that, as early as 1860, 'Delacroix already belonged to the just-emerging Impressionists'. Jerome Mellquist, 'From Delacroix to Marin', *The Sewanee Review* 53.2 (Spring 1945), 306.

Fig. 3: Eugène Delacroix, *The Lion Hunt, sketch* [*La Chasse aux lions, esquisse*], 1854. Oil on canvas, 33 4/5 x 45 1/4 inches (86 x 115 cm), Grand Palais (Musée d'Orsay), Paris

In all of these examples, Delacroix is seen wrestling both with the confluent yet mutually exclusive aims of cohesion through lyric instantaneity (which he associates with classical ideals of holism) and with the 'taste' and 'measure' of the French classical order of narrative composition associated with the school of Poussin (the American and English literary parallels to which, again ironically, he disparages for their expository excesses and resulting loss of immediacy).

With the *Lion Hunt* of 1855 (Figure 4) Delacroix revisited the theme of close, urgent conflict. The 1854 oil sketch of the same subject (Figure 3), however, shares more in directed energy (if perhaps not in rhythm) with the 1826 *Giaour* (Figure 1) – an inward-driving, vortexual motion, in particular – than it does with the *Lion Hunt* of 1861 (Figure 2).[75] The harsh directness of a single group in concerted spiral action has been tempered, in the 1861 canvas, by an expansion of its diameter (relative to the picture's edges) and an increase in the number,

---

75 Kimberley J. Smith identified a vortex-like organization of figures within and along a shared, shallow plane of space in the artist's 1826 *Giaour:* 'Though they do not touch, each horse and its rider form half of a horizontal vortex' ('"Contours of Conflict": The *Giaour* in Byron and Delacroix', *Athanor* 10 [1991], 40). In this as in all the paintings discussed here, the action moves more or less circularly, but on a single plane. The extraordinary depth and velocity of whorl among figures in these groupings are the reflection of Delacroix's efforts to 'correct' Rubens's 'confusion', such that they move within the confines of a shared and shallow plane.

Fig. 4: Eugène Delacroix, *The Lion Hunt* [*La Chasse aux lions*], 1855. Oil on canvas, 22 2/5 x 29 1/5 inches (57 x 74 cm), Nationalmuseum, Stockholm

variety, and attitudes of its participants. The group of figures still combines in a swirling clockwise frenzy; but now that wild movement is conveyed through two means – the one microcosmic, held within the scale of individual brushstrokes; the other macrocosmic, conveyed along the continuous perimeter of the *mêlée*, in a rippling and lyrical envelope of implicit contour line.[76] Attention is no longer forced inward to the heart of hostilities, but across and around the separate theatres of battle – a strategy of distraction from the singular central motion and a means of tempering, or even minimizing, that intense centrality through its repetition along the sidelines. This propulsive-implosive design, which distracts the viewer's attention from the central point, might be regarded as the painterly equivalent of litotes and praeteritio; but where Poe uses those figures to *increase* the dizzying spin of his vortex, Delacroix slows it down.

---

76 Again, the term 'vortexual' refers here to whorl-like compositional groupings that range along a single shared plane parallel to the picture plane, rather than to ones that move from a foreground into a deep background (such as J. M. W. Turner's *Light and Color (Goethe's Theory) – The Morning after the Deluge – Moses Writing the Book of Genesis* (exhibited 1843) and John Martin's *The Destruction of Pompei and Herculaneum* (1822), both in the Tate London.

Looked at in another way, the pulse of the 1861 image (Figure 2) is *drawn out over time*, through the process of the viewer's involvement in a more elaborate narrative of action. The centralized, implosive energy that drove into and among the combatants of a single, tumbling mass in the study of 1854 (Figure 3) has given way to an explosive, diasporic complex of satellites situated at left, right, top and bottom, then activated in a reasoned, balanced group of distinct episodes around a central void, like discrete gusts of violent wind revolving around the eye of a weakening storm. Thus the 1861 *Lion Hunt* (Figure 2) – however successful in its presentation of counterpoised rhythms, its resolution of compositional challenges, and its creation of formal harmonies among separate though interlinked opposing forces – replaces the 1854 study's extra-temporal whole with a complex of time-bound set-pieces. This substitution results from Delacroix's reflective consideration of the principles of classical design in the process of enlarging the scale and richness of his subject. Moreover, the span of years between these points of substitution – first twenty-eight years between the *Giaour* and the 1854 study, then six more between the study and the 1861 *Lion Hunt* – shows that Delacroix continued to struggle with the implications of an extreme, non-temporal visual language throughout his career. In the *Giaour* of 1826 his solution built concentration and power. In the 1854 *Lion Hunt* sketch that power was preserved, even increased. But when that power was brought to bear on the still later exhibition work (1861), his expansion of the vortex and division of expressive means among smaller elements of the design had the effect of taming them under the gentler yoke of a classicizing, gravity-bound (left-right-top-bottom) *contrapposto*, thereby mitigating the menace of whorling energy and, with it, the painting's effect of instantaneity.

Clearly, then, Delacroix was both drawn to and wary of extremes of expression, and at least occasionally inclined to moderate them, despite their continuing allure. These conflicting impulses do not reflect a linear trajectory in his work across decades; rather, they feed a larger, persistent struggle relived at every phase and moment of his career. They do not constitute 'stylistic development' in isolation, but an endemic conflict in all aspects of the artist's vision.

In effect, in attacking Poe's exercise in sublimity Delacroix was attacking a tendency in his own work – one which he struggled to expunge throughout his career by conforming to an onerous standard of moderation. As such, his remarks on 'The Descent into the Maelström' belong to what Michele Hannoosh has called 'the space of contradiction' in the painter's *Journal*, where two rival arts and two standards of sublimity – one of excess and one of perfect, finished proportion – are pitted against each other.[77] Delacroix does not cite Longinus's remark that 'entire accuracy runs the risk of descending into triviality, whereas in

---

77 Hannoosh, *Painting*, 66.

the grand manner, as in the possession of great wealth, something is bound to be neglected'.⁷⁸ Yet, in several places, he makes the same point: Rubens showed 'une sublime négligence' [a sublime negligence] in the execution of his *Saint Veronica* and realized his 'sublime tapestries' [sublimes tapisseries] on the death of Achilles 'sans chercher à l'infini des perfectionnements' [without striving endlessly after perfection].⁷⁹ In the same vein, he twice asserts that 'perfect proportion' is incompatible with the sublime.⁸⁰ On the other hand, in another place he seems to equate the sublime with perfection and completeness, and by implication, with a mastery of proportion.⁸¹

The lack of variety and balance – of 'taste' and 'measure' – which Delacroix deplored in Poe's story was part of a deficiency which the painter attributed to *all* 'faiseurs de romans et de pièces' [makers of novels and plays].⁸² Delacroix attributed the 'monotony' of Poe's tale to this strained consistency, this striving after a single effect. Yet Delacroix elsewhere admitted that monotony is not incompatible with the sublime.⁸³ It would appear, finally, that in rejecting Poe's intention, means, and achievement in 'A Descent into the Maelström', Delacroix was affirming a preference for the variety of life over its most singular moment.

---

78 Longinus, *On the Sublime*, 143.
79 Delacroix, *Journal*, 2:8., 3:389.
80 'une proportion trop parfaite nuit à l'impression du Sublime' [a too-perfect proportion harms the impression of the Sublime' (*Journal*, 2:207); 'le sublime est dû le plus souvent... au défaut de proportion' [the sublime is most often due to a lack of proportion] (ibid., 2:234).
81 '*Du sublime et de la perfection*. Ces deux mots peuvent sembler presque synonymes. *Sublime* veut dire tout ce qu'il y a de plus élevé; *parfait*, ce qu'il y a de plus complet, de plus achevé.' [*Of the sublime and perfection*. These two words can seem almost synonymous. *Sublime* means whatever is most elevated; *perfect*, whatever is most complete, most finished.] Ibid., 3:276.
82 'Leurs hommes sont tout d'une pièce. Il n'en est pas de cette sorte.... Il y a dix hommes dans un homme, et souvent ils se montrent tous dans la même heure.' [Their men (i. e., fictional characters) are all just one thing. There are no men like that.... There are ten men in a (real) man, and they often all reveal themselves at the same time.] Ibid., 2:288–289.
83 Ibid., 3:151. Delacroix noted that Michelangelo 'n'a point varié la physionomie de [son] terrible talent' [did not vary the physiognomy of (his) terrible talent] and argued that 'la sublime monotonie' [sublime monotony] was 'la principale qualité' [the principal quality] of Michelangelo's art. Ibid., 3:355–356.

Victoria Ferentinou
(University of Ioannina)

Re-enchanting Art in Theory and Practice:
Symbolism in Greece and Frixos Aristeus

> I am a poet or rather a philosopher expressing
> my ideas and theories through the art of painting.[1]

> Only after twenty years in 1900 did I manage
> to see the light within me. ... Another thirty seven
> years had to pass in order to see the light within darkness,
> the light of my spirit and the light of the creation of All.[2]

Abstract

This essay presents the first systematic examination of the work of the underrated Greek painter Frixos Aristeus (1879–1951). It contextualises Aristeus's oeuvre by highlighting the historical specificities of the interaction between occultism and Greek symbolism in the early twentieth century. It is specifically concerned with the ways Aristeus integrated theosophical and spiritualist ideas into his art theoretical treatise, *Light from Darkness and Darkness from Light* (mid-1930s) and his allegorical paintings. Aristeus's optic is informed by neo-romantic concepts about art as a *locus* of sacralisation and the artist as the prophet who is endowed with the task of conveying unseen realities to the wider audience. His intensive religious and epistemological searching aimed, as shall be shown, at interweaving Christian with occult ideas. In this blending, Aristeus preferred a representational art expressive of spiritual ideas that also characterised the work of other theosophically-influenced artists of his era. Through this case study the article aspires to shed light on the impact that processes of re-enchantment might have exerted upon modern visual culture in Greece.

Keywords

Religious art, Art theory, Goethe's *Zur Farbenlehre*, Theosophy, Figuration

---

1 Frixos Aristeus, 'Frixos Aristeus as an artist, painter, sculptor, philosopher and writer: Pre-introduction of Alexandros Philadelpheus', unpublished manuscript, 6, National Gallery and Alexandros Soutzos Museum Archives, Athens. All translations from Geek to English are mine, unless otherwise indicated.
2 Frixos Aristeus, 'Prologue of Light from Darkness and Darkness from Light: Analysis and Creation of the ethereal colours', unpublished manuscript, 21, National Gallery and Alexandros Soutzos Museum Archives, Athens.

In 1896, a group of theosophists from the United States visited Greece and delivered three lectures at the philological association Parnassus.[3] This visit elicited the reaction from Nikolaos Episkopopoulos, a critic writing for the Greek newspaper *Asty*. Episkopopoulos spoke in good terms about Theosophy, outlining its history and praising it 'as the evolution of all religions' because of its emphasis on altruism, mysticism, and religious tolerance.[4] On the other hand, he scorned it for its utopian visions, use of symbols and heretical concepts and pronounced that it cannot substitute Christianity. And concluded: 'Greece is not the proper *locus* for the cultivation of such novel religious ideas. We can still live alas! for long without Theosophy'.[5] This pronouncement is significant because it reflects the perspective of several intellectuals in Greece at the turn of the century. It also provides insights into Greek historiography and explains why it ignored the occult influences in the work of writers, poets, and artists working in Greece. Last but not least, it is testimony of processes of re-enchantment taking place in the country at a period of gradual industrialisation and secularisation and changes in technological infrastructure, education, social structure, and culture.[6]

Literary critics proved to be more open to the study of re-enchantment in relation to the work of certain Greek literary figures of the twentieth century.[7] Yet,

---

3 Evgenios P. Matthiopoulos, *Art Springs Wings in Sorrow: The Reception of Neo-romanticism in the Realm of Ideology, Art Theory and Art Criticism in Greece* (Athens: Potamos Publishers, 2005) (in Greek), 236.

4 Ep[iskopopoulos], N[ikolaos], 'Theosophy', *To Asty*, 21 September 1896, unpaginated (in Greek).

5 Matthiopoulos, *Art Springs Wings in Sorrow*, 237.

6 The notion of re-enchantment is connected to Max Weber's counter-thesis of disenchantment and processes of secularilisation as a cultural condition of modernity. See Max Weber, 'Science as Vocation', in *From Max Weber: Essays in Sociology*, ed. H. H. Gerth and C. Wright Mills (New York: Oxford University Press, 2007.) Re-enchantment refers to the development of alternative modes of spirituality that often weave together science and syncretic religious philosophies from the 19th century onward. Scholars revisiting the diffusion of spiritual currents outside mainstream religious institutions, such as the Catholic, Protestant, and Orthodox churches, insist that religiousness has not disappeared in the modern Western world but took other forms via modern esotericism. For the purposes of the study, 'modern esotericism' and 'occultism' will be treated as synonyms for convenience only. For the current scholarly usage of the terms, see Wouter Hanegraaff et al (eds), *Dictionary of Gnosis and Western Esotericism* (Leiden and Boston: Brill, 2006), 337–338, 887–888; Antoine Faivre, *Access to Western Esotericism* (Albany: State University of New York Press, 1994), 10–15; Wouter Hanegraaff, *New Age Religion and Western Culture: Esotericism in the Mirror of Secular Thought* (Albany: State University of New York Press, 1998*)*, 421–442. For the purposes of this essay, the term 'alternative or heterodox spiritualities' will be used as an umbrella term for non-institutionalised religious systems.

7 See for example Ritsa Frangou-Kikilia, *Angelos Sikelianos: Grades of Initiation* (Athens: Publications Pataki, 2002) (in Greek); Ourania Kaiafa (ed.), *Mysticism and Art: From Theosophy of 1900 to the "New Age"* (Athens: Etaireia Spoudon Neoellinikou Politismou kai Genikis Paideias, 2007) (in Greek); Aggela Kastrinaki, 'The Gnostic Kazantzakis', in *Kazantzakis in the 21st century*, ed. Stamatis N. Filippidis (Herakleion: Panepistimiakes Ekdoseis Kritis, 2010) (in

the academic discourse on the relationship between modern esotericism and the visual arts has been absent in Greece until 2005, when the art historian Evgenios Matthiopoulos published his study on the reception of neo-romanticism in Greece and its link to *fin-de-siècle* European occultism.⁸ Entitled Τέχνη πτεροφύει εν οδύνη [Art Springs Wings in Sorrow], this book has been the only attempt to sketch out this interaction and serves as an excellent starting point for students and academics alike. Matthiopoulos argues that it was poets and authors working as art critics who constructed the Greek discourse on art, ideology, and modern esotericism and focuses on these discursive practices. His book centres on poets and authors but does not analyse in detail the work of visual artists who were interested in occultism and/or were influenced by occult and mystical ideas, with the exception of Nikolaos Gyzis and Konstantinos Parthenis.

The question of the relevance of occult theories for early twentieth-century Greek artists merits closer scrutiny. This essay will highlight the historical complexities and cultural specificities of the interaction between occultism, and Greek art in the first decades of the twentieth century. It will most specifically be concerned with the ways Greek visual artists familiar with the symbolist discourse appropriated occult ideas and integrated them into their artistic practice and art theory. The focus will be the oeuvre of Frixos Aristeus (1879–1951), an artist largely underrated in scholarship. As will be argued, one of the primary reasons for this neglect is his often cryptic and unconventional imagery and the occult ideas embedded in his work. Furthermore, the unknown provenance of many of his canvases – they are either lost or in private collections – has greatly impeded an extensive research of his work.⁹ Yet Aristeus's artistic production reflects an almost unique tendency in twentieth-century Greek art that deserves further exploration: the sacralisation of visual art that serves as a manifestation of spiritual ideas and the divination of the artist as the *poeta vates* who experiences exaltation and transgression of one's physical limits in the process of art production. Before examining Aristeus's relationship with occultism and the post-

---

Greek), 33–76; Aggela Kastrinaki, 'Faith, Unbelief and Gnosis. Religious tendencies in the literature of the first decades of the 20th century', in *Identities in the Greek World from 1204 to the present*, ed. Konstantinos A. Dimadis (Athens: European Society of Modern Greek Studies, 2011) (in Greek), 269–80; Hristos Papazoglou, *Mystical themes and symbols in Dionysios Solomos's Carmen Seculare* (Athens: Kedros, 1995) (in Greek).

8 Matthiopoulos, *Art Springs Wings in Sorrow*.
9 On Aristeus's biographical sketches see Stellios Lydakis, *Dictionary of Greek Painters and Engravers*, vol. 4 (Athens: Melissa, 1976), (in Greek), n.p.; Evgenios Matthiopoulos, Lena Orphanou and Athina Ragia (eds), *Dictionary of Greek Artists: Painters, Sculptors, Engravers, 16th-20th century*, vol. 1 (Athens: Melissa, 1997) (in Greek), 97–8. For a recent attempt to provide a more extensive account of Aristeus's work see Antonis Saragiotis, *Greek Symbolism*, Unpublished Doctoral Thesis (Thessaloniki: University of Thessaloniki, 1999) (in Greek), 52–67.

Enlightenment project of re-enchantment, I will give a brief overview of the reception of symbolism in Greece and the ways its occult affinities were appropriated by the Greek artistic and literary circles. This is vital for understanding the cultural milieu from which Aristeus emerged and for contextualising his interweaving of art and esoteric epistemologies.

Symbolism, Occultism, and Art in Late Nineteenth and Early Twentieth-Century Greece: Revisiting the Greek Context

The interest in symbolism was stirred in Greece in the 1890s and flourished at the turn of the century in texts published in periodicals of art, culture, and literature, such as *Tehne*, *To Periodikon mas*, *Dionysus* and *Panathinaia*. The poet Kostis Palamas played a leading role in the circle of poets and authors who showed a fascination with symbolist ideas, among them Pavlos Nirvanas, Konstantinos Chantzopoulos, Ioannis Gryparis, Giannis Kampysis, Konstantinos Theotokis, Petros Zitouniatis, Ioannis Zervos and others.[10] Often characterised as macabre and decadent, these intellectuals tended to endorse modernist tendencies. Seeking for a change, both in social and cultural terms, the Greek poets and artists familiarised themselves with the work of Charles Baudelaire, John Ruskin, Friedrich Nietzsche, and Camille Flammarion but were also receptive to the occult and mystical tendencies of the French and German symbolists. Central to this shift was the leading role that the Greek poet and essayist Ioannis Papadiamantopoulos, *aka* Jean Moreas, played to the movement in France and the attraction that French culture exerted upon the Greek intelligentsia at the time.[11]

Most Greek symbolists came from low to middle class families and were opposed to the social milieu of their time. Symbolism was readily embraced since it was seen as the *locus* of the confluence of alternative and radicalised proclivities as was often the case with other European symbolisms. In Greece there were, however, other sociopolitical reasons for the endorsement of a literary and artistic movement that renounced naturalism, positivism, and materialism and embraced idealist, mystical, and neo-romantic aesthetics and poetics. The economic crisis and bankruptcy of Greece in 1893, the Greeks' defeat in the Turkish-Greek war in 1897, and the failure of Greek politicians to meet the needs of the Greek constituency created an intellectual environment in which dis-

---

10 Matthiopoulos, *Art Springs Wings in Sorrow*, 34–5. Kostis Palamas's *The Eyes of my Soul* of 1892 is considered by several scholars the first symbolist poetic collection. See Saragiotis, *Greek Symbolism*, 24.
11 See Jean Moreas, 'A Literary Manifesto – Symbolism,' *Le Figaro*, Supplément Litérraire (September 18, 1886), 150.

illusionment with materialism, rationalism, and liberalism gave way to the experimentation with decadent, anarchist, socialist, mystical, and other currents, perceived at the time as a subversive response to the *status quo*. The anxieties of the era and the changing social structure were particularly reflected upon the conflict of the two antithetical currents of tradition and modernism and the related cultural and linguistic tensions that marked the country. This conflict was mainly expressed through the so-called 'language question', that is the debate over whether to use the καθαρεύουσα [puristic language] or the δημοτική [popular or vernacular language]. In this controversy, the καθαρεύουσα was allied with mainstream culture as expressed through the State, the Academies, and the Church, whereas the δημοτική was espoused by those intellectuals willing to counter canonical discourses and institutions.[12] These intellectuals, who constituted part of the Greek spiritual vanguard, sought to regenerate Greek art and were receptive to a wide range of novel currents, such as occultism.[13] More or less Greek symbolists followed the paradigm of French and German symbolists, although in many cases the appropriation of occultism was not so explicit or dominant and developed toward different directions in Greece.

Although symbolism was not initially favoured by mainstream critics, it gradually became in vogue and was preferred in comparison to impressionism whose influence on the Greek modernists was rather anaemic.[14] The symbolist revision and reinterpretation of Greek mythology was undoubtedly one of the primary reasons for the emergence of the movement in the visual arts; it was used to reinforce the link of modern Greece with the illustrious ancient Greek civilisation and often contributed to the formulation of the nationalist discourse on Greek identity, a connection also apparent in other European symbolisms.[15] As Michelle Facos notes,

> [while] drawing inspiration from the national past might seem incompatible with the production of modern works, such a paradoxical strategy was characteristic of the way in which artists and intellectuals expressed dissatisfaction with life in the final decades of the nineteenth century.[16]

---

12 On the language question in Greece see Peter Mackridge, *Language and National Identity in Greece, 1766–1976* (Oxford: Oxford University Press, 2010).
13 For an overview see Matthiopoulos, *Art Springs Wings in Sorrow*, 33–105.
14 See Antonis Kotidis, *Modernism and Tradition in Interwar Greek Art* (Thessaloniki: University Studio Press, 1993) (in Greek), 179; Matthiopoulos, *Art Springs Wings in Sorrow*, 33–105.
15 See Kotidis, *Modernism and Tradition*, 179. See also Antonis Danos, 'Idealist "Grand Visions" from Nikolaos Gyzis to Konstantinos Parthenis: The Unacknowledged Symbolist Roots of Greek Modernism,' in *The Symbolist Roots of Modern Art*, ed. Michelle Facos and Thor J. Mednick (Surrey, England and Burlington, Vermont: Ashgate, 2015), 11–22.
16 Michelle Facos, *Symbolist Art in Context* (Berkeley: University of California Press, 2009), 10.

However, it was also via symbolism that a wide range of novel ideas, foreign to the Greek milieu, such as theories and practices drawn from occultism and the so-called 'ancient wisdom', were introduced in Greek literature and art as borrowings from Western cultural currents.

It is not, therefore, coincidental that when symbolism became known in Greece, it was defined as 'the aesthetic of mysticism', which was expected to dislodge realism and positivism.[17] For this reason, this interest often went hand in hand with the fascination with alternative modes of thought and spirituality, perceived as mystical by the contemporaries, such as Theosophy, spiritualism, psychical research, divination, and others. These uncommon for the Greek milieu pursuits were inspired by the occult preoccupations in other European countries as documented in contemporary Greek journals. Following the trend, in the 1890s lectures were delivered and articles were published by scientists and intellectuals on mesmerism and hypnotism, psychical research, and spiritualism.[18] The Greek upper class and members of the scientific and literary communities showed a curiosity for occult matters and participated in spiritualist experiments.[19] For instance, several poets and authors attended or actively participated in séances and practised hypnotism not only to test the probability of communicating with the dead but also of accessing the human mind.[20]

As was the case in other European symbolisms, there was also a mounting interest in philosophical/religious concepts drawn from the theosophical discourse current in Europe at the time. This new fascination with Theosophy shows the syncretic character of the Greek symbolists' occultism. It is mainly this syncretism and the inclusion of Greek philosophers alongside prophets from all World religions in theosophical genealogies that lured several Greek intellectuals to Theosophy.[21] Theosophical ideas appeared in Greece via the newspaper *Asty* in the early 1890s.[22] Seminal was the contribution of the politician Platon Dra-

---

17 Gryparis equated symbolism with mysticism in 1893. Episkopopoulos wrote about the aesthetic of mysticism and of symbols, which came to subvert realism. See Matthiopoulos, *Art Springs Wings in Sorrow*, 86.
18 Matthiopoulos, *Art Springs Wings in Sorrow*, 202.
19 Ibid., 204.
20 This was mainly materialised in the circle of the satirical poet Georgios Souris who organised séances at his house to summon the spirits and experimented with various occult phenomena. Ibid., 204–207.
21 See Victoria Ferentinou, 'Light from within or Light from above? Theosophical Appropriations in Early Twentieth-century Greek culture', in *Theosophical Appropriations: Kabbalah, Western Esotericism and the Transformation of Traditions*, eds. Boaz Huss and Julie Chajes (Beer Sheva: Ben-Gurion University of the Negev Press, 2016), passim.
22 In late-nineteenth-century Athens theosophical activity was not organised by a central lodge, but there is ample evidence of a growing interest in philosophical/religious concepts drawn from the contemporary theosophical discourse. The first theosophical lodge, named the Ionian Theosophical Society, was founded in Corfu in 1876, one year after the official foun-

koulis, who combined Theosophy with his utopian socialist visions.²³ A member of the Theosophical Society in England, he disseminated theosophical theories through his books and the publication of the periodical *Erevna* in Oxford between 1901 and 1908.²⁴ In order for Theosophy to be more readily embedded in Greece, he emphasised the contribution of Greek philosophers, such as Pythagoras, and linked Indian and Greek philosophers with Neoplatonism and the early Christian Fathers.²⁵ In 1894 he published the book Φως εκ των ένδον [Light from within] that outlined the ideas of Blavatsky and Anna Kingsford. This book was considered the Greek textbook of Theosophy and exerted an influence on the symbolist circles in Greece, including Frixos Aristeus and few of his colleagues.²⁶

Apart from Drakoulis, theosophical syncretism exerted a fascination over several intellectuals of neo-romantic tendencies, such as Nirvanas, Palamas, Theotokis, Nikos Kazantzakis, Zervos, and Angelos Sikelianos, showing that such preoccupation was not absent in Greece as it was usually portrayed in Greek historiography. Yet, it is also understandable why this interest has been underrated in scholarship; it is not easily traced since it was not explicitly articulated but usually integrated within other discourses. Pivotal to this is the fact that the Greek Orthodox Church strongly opposed spiritualism, Freemasonry, and Theosophy condemning them as heresies, thus impeding the wider reception of occultism in the country.²⁷ Several well-known clergymen and affiliated theologians wrote books attacking all heterodox spiritualities as evil and essentially anti-Christian,²⁸ while Freemasons and their affiliated groups, were seen as the greatest enemy of 'Orthodoxy'.²⁹ This attitude led to the careful and

---

ding of the Theosophical Society by Helena P. Blavatsky and Henry Steel Olcott in New York. This year is given by the Theosophical Society in Greece; see http://www.theosophicalsociety.gr/index.php?option=com_content&view=article&id=75&Itemid=520 (accessed 15/06/2020). See also Anonymous, 'The Theosophical Society', *The Theosophist*, vol. 1, no. 8 (May 1880), 214. For the history of Theosophy in Greece see Ferentinou, 'Light from within or Light from above?', 275-79.

23 See Panagiotis Noutsos, *The Socialist Thought in Greece from 1875 to 1974*, vol. A (1875-1907), (Athens: Gnosi, 1990) (in Greek), 62-3, 323-26.
24 Matthiopoulos, *Art Springs Wings in Sorrow*, 223.
25 Ibid., 224.
26 Noutsos, *The Socialist Thought in Greece*, 322-24.
27 *Proceedings of Orthodox Churches* 1930: 73, 127-28, 144.
28 See for example Panagiotis Trembelas, *Spiritualism in Athens* (Athens: Aderfotis Theologon o 'Sotir', 1925) (in Greek) and *Theosophy: Mystical Religion influenced by Eastern Religions* (Athens: Aderfotis Theologon o 'Sotir', 1932) (in Greek). Trembelas was a member of the Zoe Brotherhood, an Orthodox Christian group founded by monks and theologians in Greece in 1907 in order to systematically teach the Orthodox Christian doctrines and gradually reinforce the status of Christian religion within modern Greek culture.
29 Vasileios N. Giannopoulos, *Contemporary Heresies: Freemasonry* (Athens: Pataki 2002) (in Greek), 76-77.

concealed articulation of theosophical ideas in artworks, texts, and critiques that makes the work of researchers more difficult. In certain cases, this concealment was coupled with the appropriation of Theosophy for the purposes of national discourses on ethnic identity and the notion of Greekness.[30] This might explain why the Greek symbolists sought to combine Christian with pagan and esoteric systems into a synthesis termed 'occultist Orthodoxy' by Palamas.[31] The relatively late institutionalisation of Theosophy that took place in Greece in the 1920s perhaps further hindered the wider permeation of related ideas.[32] As a result, the late 1920s and the 1930s witnessed a relatively low interaction with occult theories by mostly literary figures such as Palamas or Sikelianos, who sustained an esoterically-inspired vision that endeavoured to transcend the boundaries of the arts, liberate artistic expression from positivism, and set the artist in the role of the universal magus.[33] These developments are important for shedding light on Aristeus's reception and appropriation of such trends in his theoretical and visual oeuvre in the first half of the twentieth century.

Frixos Aristeus, Symbolism, and Esoteric Epistemologies: Mystifying Artistic Creativity

The first Greek painter who showed an interest in Theosophy is very likely Nikolaos Gyzis who was teaching at the Bavarian Academy of Fine Arts in Munich from 1886 until his death in 1901.[34] Gyzis wove together classical art, the Byzantine iconographic tradition and Jugendstil.[35] His later work, after the 1880s, became more overtly religious depicting visions of angelic beings and apocalyptic sceneries through a visual language probably informed by Johann Wolfgang von Goethe's colour theories and related theosophical ideas.[36] Gyzis's

---

30 Ferentinou, 'Light from within, or Light from above?', 282–83.
31 Palamas defines 'occultist Orthodoxy' as 'the transgression of the barriers dividing "the God of the Gospel from the religion of Hellenism, and the Holy Spirit from Apollo".' See Kostis Palamas, 'Preface' in Antonios Halas, *My Correspondence with our poet Kostis Palamas* (Athens: Ideotheatron, 1999 [1934]) (in Greek), γ'. For an elaboration of this concept see Ferentinou, 'Light from within, or Light from above?', 273–75.
32 The Association of Greek Theosophical Lodges was founded in 1924, and the Theosophical Publishing House opened in 1926. In 1928 the Greek section of the Theosophical Society was recognized by the International Theosophical Society, and it is important for the history of Theosophy in Greece. See Ferentinou, 'Light from within, or Light from above?', 282–83.
33 Ibid., 286–91.
34 See Matthiopoulos, *Art Springs Wings in Sorrow*, 537–47.
35 Kotidis, *Modernism and Tradition*, 171.
36 See Spyros Petritakis, 'Through the Light, the Love: The late religious work of Nikolaos Gyzis under the light of the theosophical doctrine in Munich in the 1890s', Paper delivered at the *Enchanted Modernities: Theosophy and the Arts in the Modern World* conference organized

awareness of theosophical theories current in the 1890s in Munich might have been a source of inspiration for several of his students, including the Greek art students who were attending his classes. Frixos Aristeus was one of Gyzis's students, and he was further exposed to the work and ideas of German symbolist Franz von Stuck, who also taught at the Bavarian Academy at the time.

Aristeus was born in Athens in 1879 and showed a keen interest in painting since his childhood. From 1892 to 1897, he attended the School of Fine Arts in Athens and continued his artistic training in Munich between 1897 and 1900. He also stayed for six months in Florence to study the Great Masters of the Renaissance. After his return to Athens in 1901, he exhibited works in a style informed by German symbolism and art nouveau which was considered, in his words, 'a revolution in the arts', but received mixed reviews.[37] Having spent his small fortune to finance his studies in Munich and not being able to sell most of his work, Aristeus had to earn his living by working as an illustrator in periodicals, journals, and newspapers and occasionally as a caricaturist and established his reputation as a draughtsman with a good sense of humour.[38] Nonetheless, his most renowned work is premised on symbolism. Although Aristeus himself dismissed his allegiance to any school, he is considered by scholars as one of the few Greek artists who subscribed to the symbolist movement and whose work bridges the waning nineteenth-century academic Greek art and the emerging modernist trends in Greece.[39] Aristeus's relation to Greek modernism is, however, ambivalent, since he did not experiment so much with the formal elements of his compositions, with the exception of colour, but was more radical in his

---

by the Research Network *Enchanted Modernities: Theosophy, Modernism and the Arts, c. 1875-1960* and the University of Amsterdam, 5–27 September 2013, University of Amsterdam, The Netherlands.

37 Frixos Aristeus, *Autobiography* (Athens, 1955) (in Greek), 7-8. For example, one critic described Aristeus's work as 'vaguely symbolic' and the artist as an eccentric, while another pointed out that he is falsely credited with originality, since he is copying Arnold Böcklin. Several other critics were more sympathetic, but the artist was not wholeheartedly embraced by the art critics of his age with few exceptions. See Ion (pseudonym), 'Critical Review for the Exhibition of the Etaireia Filotexnon of 1900', *Empros*, (15 April 1900), unpaginated; Episkeptis (pseudonym), 'Critical Review for the Exhibition of the Etaireia Filotexnon of 1900', *Acropolis* (14 April 1900), unpaginated; Pavlos Matthiopoulos, 'New Greek Artists', *To Periodikon mas*, vol. 2 (1900), 294.

38 Aristeus, *Autobiography*, 36-7. He mentions the following: Athinai (Pop), Acropolis (Gavrielidis), Empros (Kalapothakis), Skrip (Eustratiadis), Astrapin (Gioldasis), Patris (Simos). He also illustrated posters advertising the publication of books such as *Dido* by Dimitrakopoulos.

39 Aristeus, *Autobiography*, 8. For a critical appraisal of Aristeus's affiliations see Miltiadis M. Papanikolaou, *History of Art in Greece*, vol. 2: *Eighteenth and Nineteenth Century* (Athens: Publications Adam, 2002) (in Greek), 225-26; Euthymia Georghiadou-Koudoura, 'Symbolism and Other Tendencies in Greek Painting 1880-1930,' *Archaiologia kai Texnes* 57 (December 1995) (in Greek), 22.

choice of subject matter. It is mainly via the iconography that Aristeus displays his borrowings from the turn- of-the century occult revival.

Aristeus must have been initially acquainted with theosophical ideas during his studies in Munich.[40] As Corinna Treitel argues, the occult movement in Germany – and in particular Munich – was popularised, available through the commercial and intellectual infrastructure, and informed the artistic avant-garde.[41] The proliferation of a mixture of neo-romantic and occult ideas in works and in the press, by his Greek colleagues in Athens, also exerted an impact upon his thinking.[42] Aristeus was working as an illustrator for several periodicals in which articles on symbolism and occultism were published, so that it is almost certain that he became acquainted with these ideas. His collaboration with the writer, playwright, and occultist Polyvios T. Dimitrakopoulos (*aka* Pol Arcas), since the beginning of the century, also seems to have played an important role. His acquaintance with Angelos Tanagras, founder and president of the Hellenic Society of Psychophysiology, whose book he illustrated, was also very likely influential.

Dimitrakopoulos, in particular, was interested in spiritualism and Theosophy as is made manifest in his prolific output. His occult preoccupations, still uncharted in historiography, inspired the production of two sociophysiological studies, as he calls them, Σιδηρά και Χρυσή Διαθήκη [The Iron and Golden Testaments, 1901], replete with theosophical references and illustrated by Aristeus. These books were translated into French and were positively reviewed by Cesare Lombroso, Max Nordau and Filippo Tommaso Marinetti among others.[43] *The Iron Testament* was also translated into English in 1931 by Stephen Gargilis, who, in his 'Introduction' highlighted the relevance of the book for his contemporaries who may gain useful insights into life and the cosmos in the aftermath of the financial crisis of 1929. Gargilis also recounts how a monk from the Mount Athos

---

40 On Aristeus's relationship with occultism see Victoria Ferentinou, 'Theosophy, Occultism and Greek Symbolism: the Case of Frixos Aristeus', *Enchanted Modernities: Theosophy and the Arts in the Modern World*, 1rst International Conference organized by the Research Network Enchanted Modernities: Theosophy, Modernism and the Arts, c. 1875–1960 and the University of Amsterdam, 25-27 September 2013, University of Amsterdam; Ferentinou, 'Light from within, or Light from above?', 291–92.

41 Corinna Treitel, A *Science for the Soul: Occultism and the Genesis of the German* (Baltimore, Maryland: Johns Hopkins University Press, 2004), 125.

42 For a mapping out of these networks see Spyros Petritakis, 'Throughout the Dark, the Light: Mapping out the Networks of Theosophists in Pre- and Interwar Athens through Specific Case Studies from Nikolaos Gyzis to Frixos Aristeas', in *Esotericism, Literature and Culture in Central and Eastern Europe*, ed. Nemanja Radulović (Belgrade: Cigoja, 2008), 225–40.

43 See Pol Arcas, *Les deux Testaments (Physiologie sociale)*, trans. Henry Faignet (Paris: Editions du monde Helenique, 1908). For the positive critiques see Polyvios T. Dimitrakopoulos, *The Iron Testament* (Athens, I. Sideris, 1929) (in Greek), 5–15.

advised him to consult the book because 'light will come to ... [him] from "within and above"'.[44]

The configuration of *The Iron Testament* as a primary textbook for those seeking enlightenment by a Christian Orthodox monk is elucidating, since it is an excellent example of 'occultist Orthodoxy' dominant in certain circles in Greece in the first half of the twentieth century and most specifically in Aristeus's work. The interweaving of Christian, spiritualist, and theosophical ideas informs Dimitrakopoulos's textual production such as *Ο Πνευματισμός. Ζωή και Επίζησις* [Spiritualism: Life and Afterlife, undated], *Η Ζωή του Θανάτου: Μυθιστόρημα Πνευματιστικόν* [The Life of Death: A Spiritualist Novel, undated] and *Το Μυστικό της Ζωής* [The Secret of Life, undated]. In all cases, he discusses the concept of futurity deeming life not as a linear progression but as an eternal cycle that entails both life and death, decomposition and regeneration, also offering his theories on telepathy, telaesthesia, mesmerism, and other related phenomena. On another occasion, he himself practised spiritualism to produce literary texts via his alleged communication with the spirits of dead Greek intellectuals. Entitled *Υπερκόσμιος Παρνασσός* [Supernatural Parnassus, 1926], the anthology consists of poems dictated to the author by the spirits of deceased Greek poets while he was in trance, a statement that created a sensation among his contemporaries. In his 'Introduction' Dimitrakopoulos theorises about the nature and function of inspiration which he equates with spiritualism grounding his theory on the pseudo-scientific discourse drawn from Theosophy and *μελλοντισμός* [futurism], which he perceives as an equivalent of the science of the future, or else parapsychology.[45] Several of Dimitrakopoulos's ideas inform Aristeus's visual and textual work, as is evident in the latter's use of occult terms or concepts so that a comparative study is helpful when examining the latter's theory and paintings. Psychical research and the oeuvre of Tanagras and his circle might also have left an imprint on Aristeus's work. It was Tanagras who founded the Greek Society of Psychical Researches in 1923, the first organisation to approach such phenomena through a scientific lens.[46] The association was very active attracting in its circles many renowned Greeks of the time, among them scientists, medical doctors, and intellectuals, including the archaeologist and Aristeus's friend, Alexandros

---

44 Stephen Gargilis, 'Introduction', in Pol Arcas, *The Iron Testament*, trans. S. Gargilis (Boston: Meador Press, 1942), 12–3.
45 Polyvios T. Dimitrakopoulos, *Supernatural Parnassus: Spiritualist Studies* (Athens: Greca, 1926) (in Greek), 3–15.
46 On Tanagras see Angelos Tanagras, *My Memoirs*, edited by Foteini Palikari (Athens: Private Publication, 2016); Angelos Tanagras, *The Lost Diary: The Life and Work of the 'Father' of Greek Parapsychology through his Manuscripts*, edited by Nikolaos Koumartzis and Aremis Veloudou-Apokotou (Athens: Daidaleos, 2017).

Philadelpheus, who was a member of the association's board.[47] Tanagras's ideas were disseminated through the publication of the annual journal *Psychikai Erevnai* from 1925 onward and the organisation of the 4th international Conference of Psychophysiology in Athens in 1930. Vehemently opposing spiritualism, Tanagras collaborated with his European colleagues in appropriating scientific methodologies; for example, he conducted telepathic experiments between Athens and Paris with the help of Dr. Warcollier from the French Institut Métapsychique International. Apart from his efforts to consolidate psychical studies in Greece, Tanagras was also a literary author collaborating with the journal *Noumas* and writing books with mystical themes, such as Άγγελος Εξολοθρευτής [Angel Terminator, 1913], illustrated by Aristeus. Tanagras's belief in the power of the human mind to transcend physical boundaries and affect reality is also recurrent in Aristeus's written oeuvre. Although there is no evidence that the painter attended any of the lectures delivered at the association, it is also through his close friendship with Philadelpheus that Aristeus must have become cognisant of any new developments of psychical research in Greece.

Although Aristeus does not explicitly mention the source of any of his ideas and theories, which he configures as products of personal reflection, it was within the above networks that he shaped his esoterically-inspired notion on creativity and art as practices of mystification. There is no evidence that he joined the Greek Theosophical Society, so perhaps, like many of his Greek and European contemporaries, he was acquainted with, or had contact with Masonic Lodges in Greece. A careful survey of his writings, surviving works and illustrations reveals the infiltration and eclectic adaptation of spiritualist and theosophical themes drawn from the discourse of Greek and German symbolists, as well as from Dimitrakopoulos's occult work and Tanagras's psychical researches. For instance, Aristeus relates in his autobiography his childhood supernatural experiences, not uncommon for his generation and for other European artists of his era.[48] Aristeus further ascribes the origin of his allegorical work to this special relation to the supernatural, considering the symbol as the pictorial externalisation of the spiritual world. In a semi-religious tone that reiterates Sâr Joséphin Péladan's aesthetic, central to French symbolism, Aristeus argues that artists are the priests of art, that their objective is to elevate humanity, and that his own artwork is a hymn to God.[49] For Aristeus, art is mainly the manifestation of ideas, which, in his case, are inspired by 'supernatural forces superior to perishable matter'.[50] And he continues 'it is through the communication with immaterial

---

47 Tanagras, *My Memoirs*, 344.
48 He speaks of his premonitions and his belief in 'omens, delusions, telepathy' as well as dreams that help him foresee the future. See Aristeus, *Autobiography*, 9–11, 53.
49 Ibid., 101.
50 Ibid., 119.

worlds that I have succeeded in rendering God, the Creation and the visions of spirits'.⁵¹

Aristeus's optic is informed by neo-romantic concepts current in Europe at the time about art as a *locus* of sacralisation and the poet/artist as the prophet/magician/seer who is endowed with the task of conveying incomprehensible truths and unseen realities to the wider audience. This world is perceived as an enchanted cosmos in which artists and supernatural beings are in direct communication with the objective of giving form and shape to the intangible dimension of reality. Visual art thus becomes a perceptible manifestation of the spiritual world, a tool in transmitting messages to the viewer, according to the symbolist aesthetics as propounded in France and Germany and deployed by various contemporary artists, such as Swedish painter Hilma af Klint. Aristeus does not experiment so much with alternative epistemologies, but he evinces an intensive religious and epistemological searching aimed, as shall be shown, at interweaving Orthodox Christian with esoteric ideas, a tendency also observed in Eastern Europe at the time but which emphatically characterises the work of other Greek symbolists, such as Gyzis's later output and Parthenis's modernist oeuvre.⁵² It is this occultist and idealist understanding of art that had had an impact upon Aristeus's recasting of art theory and practice as secular mirrors of the world of ideas.

Light from Darkness and Darkness from Light

Aristeus's metaphysical and idealist worldview is attested to throughout his writings in which he articulates his belief in the existence of supernatural entities, his devotion to a superior creative principle, and his communication with mediums and witches. However, his empirical metaphysics are better integrated into his theoretical treatise entitled Φως εκ του Σκότους και Σκότος εκ του Φωτός [Light from Darkness and Darkness from Light] written in the mid-1930s and completed in 1935. Like several artists of the early twentieth century, from Wassily Kandinsky and Piet Mondrian to František Kupka and Paul Klee, Aristeus attempted to synthesise his experience as a painter and his readings on art and colour science into a corpus of art theory that is unique for Greek standards. Although his art theoretical discourse is not entirely original, it combines romantic and neo-impressionist art theories with esoteric ideas. There are two versions of his

---

51 Ibid.
52 For examples see Radulović (ed.), *Esotericicm, Literature and Culture in Central and Eastern Europe*, passim. For the Greek symbolists' interweaving of Christian (Byzantine) and esoteric motifs see Matthiopoulos, *Art Springs Wings in Sorrow*, 537-47, 577-94.

treatise: the first is shorter, more technical and published in 1935; the second is more extensive and theoretical but remains unpublished at the archives of the National Gallery in Athens.

Overall, the treatise encapsulates the theories Aristeus formulated and which, as he argues, stem from his long experience as an artist. The title, he explains, is inspired by the idea that darkness, symbolised by the colour black, generates light, represented by the colour yellow, and light (yellow) brings forth darkness (black) in an eternal cyclical motion, echoing the Orphic cosmogony as reinterpreted by Blavatsky in her *Secret Doctrine* (1888).[53] For Aristeus, it is the artist who should extract the light from darkness and thus create his artwork using black and yellow as the two elementary colours. Recalling the German romantics, Aristeus praises night and darkness admitting that he is more creative during the nocturnal hours since 'night enlightens ... [his] genius'.[54] He even points out that the colour of his zodiacal sign (Aquarius), the blue-indigo, might explain his pastime, further showing his involvement with tropes dominant in esoteric circles but not widely legitimised, such as the use of astrology to understand one's personality.[55] Grounding his work on this concept, Aristeus offers an analysis of what he calls αιθέρια χρώματα [ethereal colours] that is the bright colours of the heavens, or else prismatic colours as perceived by the human eye, in their diverse gradations. His account echoes theosophical theories on 'ether' as well as Goethe's *Zur Farbenlehre* [Theory of Colour, 1810].

Colour played a seminal role in the art theoretical discourses and practices of the romantics in the late eighteenth and early nineteenth centuries. Responding to the increasing interest of his age, Goethe considered his study on colours 'as one of his major achievements, and on occasion he intimated that he placed his scientific work on colour above his poetry'.[56] In the first half of the book Goethe presented his own findings regarding the effect of colour on the human mind and colour symbolism, while the other half is devoted to his dispute with Isaac Newton's science of Opticks that promoted 'an abstract approach to nature' closer to mathematical methodologies.[57] In contrast, Goethe adopted a humanistic approach to the study of visual phenomena betraying his Neoplatonist leanings. He, for example, considered colours 'as acts of light; its active and passive modifications', but also a 'degree of darkness' or else '*lumen opacatum*' alluding to the reception of Neoplatonist aesthetics by German Jesuit scholar

---

53 Frixos Aristeus, *Light from Darkness and Darkness from Light* (Athens, 1935) (in Greek), 7.
54 Aristeus, 'Frixos Aristeus as an artist', 7.
55 Ibid.
56 Moshe Barasch, *Theories of Art: From Winckelmann to Baudelaire*, vol. 2 (Routledge: New York and London, 2000), 270.
57 Barasch, *Theories of Art*, 271.

Athanasius Kircher.[58] Reiterating recurrent romantic conceptions of art, he further concluded that an artwork 'should be the effusion of genius, the artist should evoke its substance and form from his inmost being, treat his materials with sovereign command, and make use of external influences only to accomplish his powers'.[59] Colour is thus legitimised as 'an inner experience' that is credited with specific meaning and aesthetic responses.[60]

These notions resound throughout Aristeus's own theory of colour that evokes romanticism but further attempts to integrate Georges-Pierre Seurat's 'divisionist' theories of colour application on the surface of the canvas to accomplish chromatic harmony through the union of opposites.[61] Another likely source is Rudolph Steiner's lectures on light and darkness and his reflections on Goethe's theoretical studies on colour theory with which Aristeus might have been familiar.[62] Steiner, a theosophist who founded his own esoteric school, Anthroposophy, in 1913, dedicated many years to the exploration of the German philosopher's colour theory, which he edited, prefaced, and published as volumes 3 and 4 of *Einleitung Zu Goethes Naturwissenschaftliche Schriften* [Goethean Science or Nature's Open Secret, 1883-1897]. In this way, he made available the idealist, in his opinion, reflections, and findings of the illustrious philosopher in the late nineteenth century at a time when colour was the primary formal element of experimental art. It is also noteworthy that Steiner revisited scientific practices, which he deemed as a form of idealism, and it is through this prism that he construed Goethe's theories. This idealism also informs Aristeus's work.

It can be fairly argued that Aristeus's treatise reflects his familiarity with theosophical theories on art and colours current in Munich in the late 1890s and in 1911, when he briefly visited the city, although there is high probability that his knowledge was more or less superficial.[63] It is also probable that he had read, or was acquainted with Goethe's theories on colour symbolism via Gyzis or Steiner's editions of Goethe's work. Aristeus's allegiance to a confluence of

---

58 Goethe, *The Theory of Colour* (1810) quoted in Barasch, *Theories of Art*, 271. In the latter instance, Goethe refers to a concept mentioned in Athanasius Kircher's *Ars magna lucis et umbrae* (Rome, 1646) in which colours are described as 'the children of light and darkness'.
59 Goethe, *The Theory of Colour* (1810) quoted in Barasch, *Theories of Art*, 274.
60 Barasch, *Theories of Art*, 274.
61 The concept of the union of opposites as vital for the art of painting features in Charles Henry's 'The Chromatic Circle' (1888) and Seurat's writings and reflect 'the relationship of Neoimpressionism to late-nineteenth-century scientific transcendentalism'. In particular Seurat wrote: 'Art is Harmony. Harmony is the Analogy of contrary and similar elements of tone, of color, and of line'. See Joshua C. Taylor, *Nineteenth-Century Theories of Art* (Berkeley: University of California Press, 1987), 530-531.
62 Rudolph Steiner, *Genesis: Lecture V, Secrets of the Bible Story of Creation*, Munich, 21 August 1910, Rudolph Steiner Archive accessed June 3 2020, http://wn.rsarchive.org/Lectures/GA/GA0122/19100821p02.html.
63 On his visit in Munich in 1911 see Aristeus, *Autobiography*, 40-2.

occult and symbolist aesthetics is also manifest in his brief reference to synaesthetic theories as were famously expressed by French symbolist poet Charles Baudelaire in his poem 'Correspondances' [Correspondences, 1857].[64] Aristeus writes for example: 'the adjectives sweet, sour, bitter applied to colours should not surprise us.... there is correspondence between sensations, and we often characterise a perfume as sweet, strong, delicate, sour, or heavy, and so forth'.[65] Nevertheless, he investigates neither synaesthesia nor its importance for envisioning the astral body as was articulated in the well-known book *Thought-Forms* (1905) by theosophists Annie Besant and Charles W. Leadbeater. Aristeus, however, develops the theosophical idea that 'thoughts are things'.[66] For him everything consists of matter, even spirit, so that the invisible dimension of reality is actually 'a product either of excessive light or absolute darkness'.[67] In this way, Aristeus spiritualises matter rather than depriving spirit from matter, thereby attempting to make visible the usually unseen, immaterial dimensions of the cosmos in line with the occult aesthetics of symbolism and early abstraction.

His neo-romantic approach is also evinced in the 'Epilogue' of his published book, when he views his colour theory through an esoterically-inspired cosmological vision. Creation, he argues, is the synthesis of all elements of nature that come together through eros, the centripetal force that unites everything in the universe. In this synthesis, life and death co-exist as expressed through the two main ethereal colours, black and yellow, and their transformation through light from one colour of the spectrum to the other, until black becomes first yellow and then white, and white becomes black in a perpetually self-transforming interplay of oppositions.[68] The concluding remark echoes Dimitrakopoulos's futuristic theories: 'it is through colours that it is ascertained that creation does not have any beginning nor end ... the end produces the beginning and the beginning the end'.[69]

In the unpublished versions, Aristeus articulates several other ideas of theosophical origin. Religion had been the motivating force of art for millennia, he argues, but nowadays science has taken its place.[70] This is inevitable, since it

---

64 See Charles Baudelaire, 'Correspondences' (1857) in *Flowers of Evil*, trans. by James McGowan (Oxford: Oxford University Press, 1998), 18–9. On an introduction to synaesthesia see Cretien van Campen, *The Hidden Sense: Synaesthesia in Art and Science* (Cambridge: Massachusetts: MIT Press, 2008).
65 Aristeus, *Light from Darkness and Darkness from Light*, 26.
66 Annie Besant and Charles Webster Leadbeater, *Thought-Forms* (London: The Theosophical Publishing House), 1905, 16 accessed June 17 2020, http://www.gutenberg.org/files/16269/16269-h/16269-h.htm.
67 Aristeus, *Light from Darkness and Darkness from Light*, 33.
68 Ibid., 45–8.
69 Ibid., 47.
70 See Frixos Aristeus, 'My ideas and thoughts. From my unpublished treatise *Light from*

follows the universal law of progress and change that demands a new art which would express the imminent new age. For Aristeus, predecessors of the art of the future are Richard Wagner in music, Arnold Böcklin in painting, and Jules Verne in literature.[71] In this passage, Aristeus calls Wagner a μελλοντιστής [futurist] and then admits that he, likewise, had been a futurist for thirty-seven years. Aristeus's notion of μελλοντισμός [futurism] echoes Dimitrakopoulos's 'Introduction' in *The Supernatural Parnassus* where he equates futurism with spiritualism. Although the same term was also used in Greek to signify the homonymous artistic movement, Aristeus's 'futurism' does not show any allegiance to the movement but is employed to denote his double alignment to science and metaphysics and the theosophical effort to weave them together.

His vision for a new art further echoes an occult perspective on the arts as a mirror of the spiritual world. He pinpoints:

> The artist should be a visionary and depict the essence of things, rather than their material form, seeing through his soul. For this reason, he should collaborate with nature and with the mysteries of the infinite universe. It is through the communication with these natural and cosmic forces that the artist would be able to recreate the world in his work.[72]

The extract summarises romantic theories about the relationship of the artist and nature and the ultimate production of the artwork as a crystallisation of this collaboration. Nature is configured in terms of direct, emotive experience and as a *locus* of sacred forces. It is the artist, who has the power to comprehend these mysteries through 'his spiritual eye', his psyche, and is hence capable of formulating afresh reality as representation. By privileging inner vision, Aristeus echoes not only the romantics but also Kandinsky's theories in *Concerning the Spiritual in Art* (1911) that sought alternative modes of representation to give shape and colour to spiritual, emotional, and moral truths, thereby putting forward new laws for the art of the future. It cannot be ascertained to what extent Aristeus read or knew the art theories produced by other contemporary European artists, but his treatise dialogues more or less explicitly with symbolist poetics and aesthetics, and occult sources that influenced early abstract artists, offering a Greek response to contemporaneous art theoretical discourses.

Although Aristeus seems to have assimilated several of the theosophical and spiritualist ideas circulating in the first quarter of the twentieth century in Europe and in Greece, his vision did not involve formal experimentation with abstraction, as was the case with Kandinsky and other European colleagues inspired by occultism, such as Mondrian, Malevich, Hilma af Klint, Kupka, and others. As

---

Darkness and Darkness from Light: Pre-Introduction', unpublished manuscript, 7, National Gallery and Alexandros Soutzos Museum Archives, Athens.
71 Aristeus, 'My ideas and thoughts', 8.
72 Ibid., 10.

shall be demonstrated below, he rather preferred an art based on concrete forms portraying naturalistically depicted figures, even if he wished to convey abstract ideas or metaphysical truths. As has been shown, these ideas were often drawn from symbolist discourse and symbolism remained a constant in his work untill his death. Despite his experimentation with colour theories, his insistence on correct drawing shows that he was not keen on moving from the mostly representational symbolism to the abstract forms of expressionism.[73] Aristeus was, after all, dismissive of modernist currents arriving in Greece, such as cubism, futurism, and surrealism, which he considers symptomatic of the decadence of humanity and its degeneration, echoing Nordau's theories.[74] It is thus only figurative art that can give form to his enchanted visions and further explore the possibilities of a spiritual art liberated from the constraints of external mimesis but in accordance with institutionalised Theosophy that prized representational art as an optical reflection of a transcendental reality.[75] Not coincidentally, the preference for a representational art expressive of spiritual ideas also characterised the work of other theosophically-influenced artists, such as Finnish painter Akseli Gallen-Kallela and Belgian painter and theosophist Jean Delville. Although symbolist art has been seen as the 'most fertile aesthetic source for abstract artists' containing the 'seeds' for non-representational art, it did not necessarily lead to non-figuration, an indication that symbolism was not a monolithic art and literary movement but entailed diverse responses to contemporary occult developments in different cultural contexts.[76]

Toward an Art of Enchantment

Most of Aristeus's artworks were premised on mythological or religious themes, often reappropriated to convey the harmonious fusion of Christianity with ancient Greek religion in a syncretic mode reminiscent of Blavatsky's teachings about the existence of one 'wisdom-religion', whose secret doctrine pervades all world

---

73 It is noteworthy that Aristeus characterises several of his works as 'expressionist compositions', revealing his acquaintance with the German avant-garde. Nevertheless, he uses the term freely just to express his colour experimentation. See Aristeus, 'Frixos Aristeus as an artist', 9–10.
74 He was perhaps familiar with these theories via Dimitrakopoulos. See Aristeus, *Autobiography*, 103–4.
75 See Tessel Bauduin, 'Abstract Art as "By-Product of Astral manifestation": The Influence of Theosophy on Modern Art in Europe', in *Handbook of the Theosophical Current*, eds. Olav Hammer and Mikael Rothstein (Leiden: Brill, 2013), 429–52.
76 Maurice Tuchman, 'Hidden Meanings in Abstract Art', in *The Spiritual in Art: Abstract Painting 1890–1985*, ed. Maurice Tuchman (Los Angeles: Los Angeles County Museum of Art, 1986), 37.

religions.⁷⁷ *Απόλλων-Χριστός* [Apollo-Christ, c. 1902], *Ο Μέγας Διδάσκαλος* [The Great Teacher, c. 1900s], *Ωδή στον Ήλιο* [Ode to the Sun, c. 1900], *Ο Αρχάγγελος Μιχαήλ, Ψυχοπομπός* [Archangel Michael, Psychopomp, undated], *Σοφία και Πνεύμα* [Wisdom and Spirit, undated] are some examples. Although he also executed more mundane paintings from landscapes and portraits to genre paintings, his symbolist works were informed by modern esotericism and centred around topics such as the union and complementarity of opposites, or the constant battle between light and darkness, life and death, or male and female. Finally, Aristeus himself confesses that he created a group of artworks dictated, or suggested, to him by supersensible entities that can be mainly appreciated from a symbolist angle.⁷⁸

In this essay I will look at examples that were analysed by Aristeus himself in his unpublished writings, since his pictorial work was utilised retrospectively as a form of illustration for his theories. The first example is *Έρως Εσταυρωμένος* [The Crucified Eros] (Fig. 1), a work executed circa 1900.⁷⁹ The God of Love is portrayed as a fat child with long hair and huge wings crucified on a cross while gazing with sorrow on a ground filled with luxuriant vegetation. His head is adorned with orange flowers, a symbol of the regeneration of nature and fertility and a likely allusion to Sandro Botticelli's famous painting *Primavera* (Spring) (c. 1480) in which the fecundating powers of nature are celebrated within an orange orchard. The crucifixion of a figure other than Jesus Christ recalls vividly Felicien Rops's *The Temptation of Saint Anthony* (1878), in which the Saint is forced to encounter a blasphemous image of a naked woman disturbingly crucified in place of Jesus, who is usurped by a demonic creature. Meaningfully, Rops substitutes the inscription of 'Jesus' on the top of the cross with that of 'Eros', a subversive gesture which was most likely known to Aristeus. Aristeus creates his own image of the crucifixion of Love by conflating pagan and Christian iconography in a unique – for Greek standards – depiction of the principle of love allied with both fertility and death. Aristeus's affinities with European symbolists is also evident in Eros's hypnotic gaze that bears similarities to the most morbid and dark examples of visual art by von Stuck and Belgian symbolist Fernand Khnopff.

When reinterpreted by Aristeus three decades later, the obscure image of the winged God of Love crucified on a cross exemplifies his theory that Love is the mediating principle that unites death and life. Adopting the cyclical worldview of the theosophists rather than the linear of Christianity, he argues that life and death constitute the circle of eternity and of immortality and also the world of

---

77 Helena P. Blavatsky, *The Secret Doctrine: The Synthesis of Science, Religion and Philosophy*, vol. I, (London: The Theosophical Publishing Company, 1888).
78 Aristeus, *Autobiography*, 120–23.
79 Aristeus, 'My ideas and thoughts', 14.

Fig. 1: Frixos Aristeus, *The Crucified Eros* (Έρως Εσταυρωμένος), c. 1900, dimensions unknown, Private Collection. Reproduced from *Pinakotheke*, vol. 1, no.9 (1901), 197.

nothing, from which emanates the manifestation of life.[80] 'Life is death in action' and 'Death is life inactive', he proclaims.[81] Transgressing the boundaries between life and death, Aristeus concludes that Eros and death actually constitute the same principle.[82] This focus is pervasive in his work, as we have seen, since the first decade of the twentieth century. The idea that the boundaries between life and death are vague recall neo-romantic works by Nirvanas, Episkopopolos, or Kampysis but also Dimitrakopoulos's treatise *The Life of Death*. It is also connected to Aristeus's reception and appropriation of esoteric spirituality and the contemporary theosophical discourse.

A second work illustrating Aristeus's theory is *Τίποτε* [Nothing] (Fig. 2), most likely produced in the 1930s. The painting represents a gigantic oval-shaped ring

---

80 Ibid., 11–14.
81 Ibid., 12.
82 Ibid., 13.

hovering above a mound of skulls, which is identified with the large numerical figure of zero symbolising the pervasiveness of non-being and death.[83] Aristeus relates how the image was inspired: in one of his visions he saw within darkness a blue spherical nebula, identified as nothingness, self-producing a second nebula in the form of the number one and recognised as being.[84] Then the zero-shaped nebula expanded and filled in the universe forming infinity and the cycle of immortality, so that it was no longer visible.[85] Another nebula that simultaneously corresponded to the digits one and zero appeared, and the two nebulae were fused together, giving birth to the cosmos.[86] Aristeus identifies 'zero' with the feminine principle, which created from itself the masculine principle, conceptualised as the digit one. It is from the latter that the second feminine principle was created and then was impregnated, bringing to life Eros, the God of Love and Death, and the creative principle of All.[87] Aristeus's explanatory text bears striking resemblances to Blavatsky's passage from *The Secret Doctrine* (1888), where she explains the universality of the symbol of the egg and its meaning in cosmogonic myths all over the world;[88] it also reflects his allegiance to Orphism, a philosophical current popular with Greek poets such as Sikelianos in the interwar years.[89]

Aristeus's text provides an insight into a third work produced in 1946, *Η Δημιουργία* [The Creation] (Fig. 3), which should be read as a companion piece to *Nothing*. This time he gives form to the moment of the conjunction of the masculine and the feminine principles to create the world, which he depicts as an embraced couple forming a sphere rotating in the starry universe.[90] This is a provocative image of Creation that was likely drawn from theosophical narratives of the genesis of the cosmos and recalls Blavatsky's concept of the creative principle as androgynous or double-sexed, containing within itself both male and female sexes. Aristeus's reliance upon the theosophical conception of the divine principle is, moreover, attested to in his text, where he argues that the first principle is simultaneously feminine and androgynous and generated the world through the conjunction of contraries, a radical concept for an Orthodox

---

83 Aristeus, 'Prologue of Light from Darkness', 21–22.
84 Ibid., 22.
85 Ibid.
86 Ibid., 23.
87 Ibid., 27.
88 Blavatsky, *The Secret Doctrine*, 359–368. It is most likely that Aristeus was acquainted with these theories through Drakoulis's, *Light from within*, since his description calls to mind certain passages from the aforementioned work.
89 On Sikelianos's Orphism, see Frangou-Kikilia, *Angelos Sikelianos-Degrees of Initiation*, 117–191.
90 Aristeus, 'Prologue of Light from Darkness', 27.

Fig. 2: Frixos Aristeus, *Nothing* (Τίποτε), c. 1930s, dimensions unknown, Private Collection.

Christian.[91] Drakoulis's *Light from within* might be a source here, since the Greek theosophist devoted chapters on divinity as an androgynous entity in his book.[92]

The two aforementioned artworks are unique in terms of iconography and style, since they deviate from modern Greek art and its leanings – classical, Byzantine, and folk art – but they do not appear to be inspired by the symbolist imagery in other European countries. No iconographic parallels have been traced, and it is fair to attribute their eccentric imagery to Aristeus himself. Both works evince a pantheistic view of the world, which is not created by a masculine God but is the product of the reconciliation of two complementary opposite principles that comprise a totality, the cosmos. These 'heretical' images feature in black-and-white reproductions in Aristeus's archive, but their provenance is today unknown. Yet, they constitute the most intriguing examples of the painter's allegiance to a spiritual tradition that is nourished by the interweaving of pagan and occult cosmogonies, but it is not totally removed from the cultural climate of interwar Greece, as can be ascertained in the work of Sikelianos or Kazantzakis. According to the artist, they also provide two excellent examples of the application of his colour theories to his practice: in both cases the allegorical content is reinforced by the use of the two most important colours according to his art theory, black and yellow, to indicate the interplay of being and non-being, life and

---

91 Ibid., 29, 31.
92 Platon Drakoulis, *Light from within* (Athens, Ideotheatron, 2000) (in Greek), 173–76.

Fig. 3: Frixos Aristeus, *The Creation* (Η Δημιουργία), 1946, dimensions unknown, Private Collection. Reproduced from Frixos Aristeus, *Autobiography*, Athens, 1955 (in Greek), upaginated.

death. In other words, form and content are seen as inseparable in the project of representing transcendental visions of cosmogony.

Another relevant work is a pastel he executed in 1949 that combines Christian, classical, and occult references into a distinctly religious image, entitled *O Ων* [The Being or God] (1949) (Fig. 4). The Greek word, which Aristeus uses to signify Divinity, is Ο Ων, whose suffix denotes a masculine rather than a feminine principle. It is very likely that Aristeus derived his title from Drakoulis's chapter on 'Divine Essence' in *Light from within*, where the author remarks that the words ωόν, meaning the egg, and ο ων, signifying existence, are composed of the same letters, both actually revealing the same essence from which the world was generated.[93] Although Drakoulis speaks of divine essence in gender-neutral terms, in this instance Aristeus visualises the Divine as a masculine principle reminiscent of both classical images of Zeus or Poseidon and Byzantine portrayals of Christ Pantocrator (the Almighty). Aristeus gives a detailed account of this image in his *Autobiography* proudly admitting that it is both a product of his colour theory and of his vision of the Divine:

> Initially I made a geometrical drawing: a circle within a square. Within the circle I put the three primary colours, red, yellow and blue, next to each other and vertically, which in my

---

93 Drakoulis, *Light from within*, 50.

Fig. 4: Frixos Aristeus, *The Being or God* (Ο Ων), 1949, pastel, 70 x 70 cm, National Gallery and Alexandros Soutzos Museum, Athens.

opinion constitute light and darkness. Darkness, namely black, originating from the fusion of the above colours, was put around the central circle… [and] around the square I painted a circle that radiates luminous yellow rays upon a black background, because, as I argue, light brings forth darkness and darkness [brings forth] light in an infinite sequence.[94]

Aristeus continues his description with the most remarkable confession: he was not satisfied with the image at first and subsequently felt ill. He thought that God punished him because he dared to portray Divine existence. But through praying and entreaty, God revealed His form to him and after a few sketches he managed to depict the Divine image.[95] Aristeus's treatment of the subject is revelatory, since he not only confesses his religious beliefs but also weaves together theosophical with Christian motifs in a paradoxical – for Greek standards – artistic visualisation of the supreme creative principle. To give form to the Divine, he further binds together the alchemical image of the 'squaring of the circle', a symbol of the philosophers' stone and of material and spiritual perfection, with his

---

94 Aristeus, *Autobiography*, 120–21.
95 Ibid.

conceptualisation of the three primary colours and the co-existence of light (yellow) and darkness (black) as signifiers of totality.[96]

Reflecting on the above images, it could be argued that all four works, although spanning the 1900s to the 1940s, are placed by Aristeus within the same thematic and echo his lifelong experimentation with and exploration of heterodox spiritual ideas current in Greece in the first decades of the twentieth century. It is significant that the artist himself considers works of his youth alongside works of his maturity and formulates a personal philosophy that seems static and constantly informed by the turn-of-the-century symbolist discourse on art and spirituality. If, however, put into context, it is equally important that the Greek section of the Theosophical Society was founded in Greece in the late 1920s, more broadly disseminating its doctrines, and that poets read in theosophical sources, such as Palamas and Sikelianos, spoke more overtly about the fruitful conjunction between paganism and Christianity in the 1920s and 1930s.[97] Moreover, what Greek scholars call 'neo-symbolism' was still in vogue in the country until the Second World War, a revival specific to the Greek political and social environment and the identitarian politics involved in contemporaneous artistic discourses.[98] Aristeus's reliance upon symbolism and his re-enchanting strategies should, therefore, be understood within this context taking also into account his conservative politics and his artistic self-isolation.[99] It is perhaps because of his individuality, his distantiation from avant-garde circles in the interwar years, and his rather pronounced esoteric spirituality that his theoretical text and explicitly occult paintings lacked visibility in artistic circles exerting no influence on his contemporaries. Aristeus was undoubtedly marginalised for many reasons, and his revitalisation of religious painting removed from the Byzantine tradition in terms of dogma and imagery did not prove helpful. Yet to this day his oeuvre still provides an interesting example of the wedding between visual art and esoteric epistemologies in the Greek context.

---

96 On such images see Michael Maier, *Atalanta Fugiens* (1618), in Stanislas Klossowski De Rola, *The Golden Game; Alchemical Engravings of the Seventeenth Century* (London: Thames and Hudson, 1997), 81, 100.
97 This was discussed at length in Ferentinou, 'Light from within, or Light from above?'.
98 See Saragiotis, *Greek Symbolism*, 2; Kotidis, *Modernism and Tradition*, 220–240.
99 Kotidis correctly remarks that Aristeus's work remains relatively unchanged throughout his career; see Antonis Kotidis, *Nineteenth-Century Painting* (Athens: Ekdotiki Athinon, 1995) (in Greek), 41. Aristeus's highly subjective perspective toward art and the negative reviews he received might have led him into a more individualistic imagery. The artist poignantly remarks that his works were revolutionary for both the public and his colleagues throughout his career, but he had not been affected by such responses, since he prefers to retain his individuality and create his art according to his 'nature' and 'personal ideas'; see Aristeus, 'My ideas and thoughts', 16.

In Conclusion

As has been demonstrated in this essay, Aristeus's pictorial and verbal work provides insights into the ways the sacralisation of art was realised in the framework of the symbolist movement in Greece and its deployment of heterodox discourses of spirituality. In this, Greek symbolism followed the trends of European symbolism that was a transnational movement with geographical diversity. Aristeus's relationship with alternative forms of religiosity admittedly impacted his oeuvre that incorporated a literary and philosophical vocabulary on enchantment derived from Theosophy, spiritualism, psychical research, astrology, and other occult currents. His visual work was not a mere illustration of such concepts but offered the impetus for the formulation of an iconography in which the spheres of the sacred and the secular were no longer clearly demarcated. This transgression of boundaries was typical of the romantic poet-genius whose vocation was to decipher the great enigma of life and convey his own enchanted visions of the world. Aristeus circulated in artistic and literary circles in which various occult ideas proliferated, and although mere use of occult themes is not proof of personal faiths, it was made manifest that he was receptive to the theosophical and spiritualist ideas current at the time, producing an art theoretical text and works informed by these discourses. It was, among others, mainly his very affinities with occultism that did not facilitate a wider visibility of his work. As a result, Aristeus's paradigm did not find any followers in the visual arts or art theory, further revealing the complexities and particularities of the Greek context.

Aristeus contributed to the shaping of Greek symbolism with an eccentric body of work undervalued by his contemporaries. Yet, it is exactly this differentiation from the canon that merits closer examination to shed light on the impact that alternative spiritualities and processes of secularisation and re-enchantment might have exerted upon modern visual culture in Greece. Aristeus's case is another testimony of the wider dissemination of occult currents not only in the metropolitan centres but also in the periphery of Europe; it further exemplifies the idiosyncratic relationship between art and secular modes of spirituality in the modern era in ways that demand a careful revision of art history's grand narratives on modernity's disenchantment and pictorial art's self-referentiality.

PhD Projects

Tim van Gerven
(University of Amsterdam)

Scandinavism: Wiring Nationalism in the North

Scandinavism. Overlapping and Competing Identities in the Nordic World, 1770–1919
Award date: 1 July 2020
451 pp.

Keywords
Scandinavism, romantic nationalism, pan-nationalism, cultural memory, cultivation of culture

Pan-nationalism is one of the intellectual products of romantic thinking that in my experience has been most poorly understood by modern scholarship. Methodological nationalism rears its ugly head: in most cases the pan-national movements failed to realize the (political) pan-nation and they accordingly represent a 'road not taken' in the history of modern state formation, as Joep Leerssen has phrased it.[1] In the definition of the American historian Louis L. Snyder, the pan-movements were 'politico-cultural movements seeking to enhance and promote the solidarity bound together by common or kindred language, cultural similarities, the same historical traditions, and/or geographical proximity. They postulate the nation writ large in the world's community of nations'.[2] When confining ourselves to Europe, the ethnolinguistic argument seems to have been guiding Pan-Germanism, Pan-Slavism, Pan-Latinism, Celticism, Illyrianism, Turanism, and Greater Netherlandism; all these movements shared the goal of bringing geographically-dispersed groups speaking related languages or dialects closer together, be it politically or otherwise.[3] Overgrown and largely abandoned, these pan-national roads appear to be invisible from the perspective of the present-day map of nations; the subject has for this reason garnered only meagre attention from students of nationalism. In my

---

[1] Joep Leerssen, *National Thought in Europe. A Cultural History* (Amsterdam: Amsterdam University Press, 2006), 18.
[2] Louis L. Snyder, *Macro-Nationalisms. A History of the Pan-Movements* (Westport and London: Greenwood Press, 1984), 5.
[3] For an introduction to these various movements and suggestions for further reading, see the thematic articles in the second volume of the *Encyclopedia of Romantic Nationalism in Europe*, 2 vols., ed. Joep Leerssen (Amsterdam: Amsterdam University Press, 2018) or visit the website: www.ernie.uva.nl.

dissertation on Scandinavism, I show that there is more to this particular pan-national movement than a preconceived story of political failure. Pan-Scandinavian cultural activism would have a significant impact on the trajectories which the separate national movements in Denmark, Norway, and Sweden were to take. Simultaneously, Scandinavism proved to be highly successful in creating an overarching Scandinavian identity that suffused and overlapped the individual national identities.

Beyond Political Failure

Fig. 1: Coat of Arms, Schleswig-Holstein.

Scandinavism, as a proper movement, emerged from student circles in the 1830s and 1840s and continued to have a great appeal, primarily, but not exclusively, in the intellectual milieu, during the next two decades. Visions of pan-Scandinavian political cooperation, in whichever shape or form, were grounded on ideas of common tribal origins and shared culture, history, language, and religion. Denmark's conflict with the burgeoning national movement in Schleswig and Holstein served as a catalyst for discussions on a future Scandinavian union, which was seen as a necessary protective shield against possible Prussian (or Russian) aggression. Despite the celebration of pan-Scandinavian brotherhood and solidarity perpetuated by decades of Scandinavist activism, Norway and Sweden did not offer Denmark any meaningful military support once the Second Schleswig War broke out in 1864. The – for Denmark – traumatic outcome of the war – both duchies were lost in their entirety – did much to break the back of political Scandinavism according to the customary portrayal of the movement in national histories and encyclopaedia-entries. The older literature focusing on Scandinavism contributed to sustaining this image of a failed political project.

These monographs by Åke Holmberg (published in 1946), John Sanness (1959), and Henrik Becker-Christensen (1981) are furthermore affected by their limited thematic, temporal, and geographical approach, as they focus primarily on political Scandinavism during the decades of the Schleswig question in Sweden, Norway, and Denmark respectively.[4]

The main problem with the narrative of political failure lies in the fact that it obscures the significant impact of Scandinavism outside the realm of politics. Over the last decade and a half, scholars have started to take an interest in the cultural implications of Scandinavist thought. In her dissertation from 2008, Ruth Hemstad minutely dissects the resurgence of Scandinavist activism in the decade around 1900, showing that the movement had a prolonged ideological attraction after 1864, thus laying strong foundations for the Scandinavian cooperation that has existed until this very day. *En passant* Hemstad demonstrates that dreams of a political union ultimately foundered in 1905 with the break-up between Norway and Sweden – four decades later than commonly accepted.[5] That the investigation of Scandinavism is a highly dissertation-driven affair is once more exemplified by Kari Haarder Ekman, who in her doctoral thesis from 2010 convincingly argues that the Modern Breakthrough – the literary movement that propelled Scandinavia into the limelight of the world republic of letters – can be understood as yet another manifestation of cultural Scandinavism. Most importantly, by turning Scandinavia into a shared literary space, the otherwise marginal individual languages could enlarge their cultural capital on the world stage, which contributed to the success of such authors as Ibsen and Strindberg.[6] That Scandinavism indeed impacted a wide-ranging number of different fields is furthermore illustrated by two anthologies on the subject that came out in 2012 and 2018, of which the chapters address such diverse subjects as art, literature, media, science, church life, women's rights, and popular culture.[7]

---

4 Åke Holmberg, *Skandinavismen i Sverige vid 1800-tallets mitt (1843–1863)* (Göteborg: Elanders Boktryckeri, 1946); John Sanness, *Patrioter, Intelligens og skandinaver. Norske reaksjoner på skandinavismen før 1848* (Oslo: Universitetsforlaget, 1959); Henrik Becker-Christensen, *Skandinaviske drømme og politiske realiteter – den politiske skandinavisme 1830–1850* (Aarhus: Arusia – Historiske skrifter, 1981).
5 Ruth Hemstad, *Fra Indian Summer til nordisk vinter. Skandinavisk samarbeid, skandinavisme og unionsoppløsningen* (Oslo: Akademisk Publisering, 2008).
6 Kari Haarder Ekman, *'Mitt hems gränser vidgades.' En studie i den kulturella skandinavismen under 1800-talet* (Göteborg & Stockholm: Makadam Förlag, 2010).
7 Magdalena Hillström and Hanne Sanders eds., *Skandinavism. En rörelse och en idé under 1800-talet* (Stockholm & Göteborg: Makadam Förlag, 2012), and Ruth Hemstad, Jes Fabricius Møller and Dag Thorkildsen eds., *Skandinavismen. Vision og virkning* (Odense: Syddansk Universitetsforlag, 2018).

Cultural Incubator and Significant Other

Combined, the studies discussed above have done much to revaluate Scandinavism's multifarious and highly impactful position in nineteenth-century life. One vital aspect of Scandinavism that to my mind had nonetheless remained underexposed concerned the entanglement between Scandinavism on the one hand and the three individual national movements on the other. How did Scandinavian identity formation interact with the various nationally-specific manifestations of cultural nationalism? That was my main research question. I found that Scandinavism wired the nation-building projects in Denmark, Norway, and Sweden on a very fundamental level, stimulating the articulation of well-defined national identities in both a positive and a negative way.

On the positive side, I build on Haarder Ekman's conceptualization of Scandinavia as a literary space by widening the scope and defining Scandinavia as a cultural sphere, a concept which pairs the infrastructure of the emerging Scandinavian public sphere to a shared repertoire for cultural cultivation. The elementary components of this common cultural repertoire are primarily memory sites from Scandinavian history. Historicism – the use of history in the formulation of collective identities – was the one area where national and Scandinavian identity-making would most fruitfully intersect. Norse Antiquity and the Viking Age were considered a shared historical mainspring and a Golden Age, offering ample material for narratives of brotherhood and rapprochement. Arguably more interesting is the inventive way in which cultural producers dealt with memories from Early Modernity – an era that was notoriously tainted by almost incessant inter-Scandinavian warfare and conflict. Novelists, poets, painters, and others engaged in an activity which I have termed the 'defusing of memory sites': stories of conflict were creatively turned into stories of reconciliation by highlighting the unnaturalness of war between brother nations or by introducing an alternative enemy (Germans, Russians, *Snaphanerne*, a seventeenth-century, pro-Danish guerrilla movement) or a social opposition that exceeded the national conflict. Such narrative interventions made it possible to celebrate national achievements and national heroes without upsetting the harmonious relations with the Scandinavian neighbours, while enforcing both strains of identity – the national and the pan-national – in the process. In its capacity of cultural sphere, Scandinavia accordingly functioned as a cultural incubator: the realization that they were embedded in a larger and more prestigious cultural community provided the individual nations with a greater cultural self-confidence, giving them the opportunity to boast a stronger profile towards the outside world.

On the other side 'Scandinavia' also stimulated nationalist self-silhouetting in a negative sense. Especially from the Norwegian perspective – the culturally less-developed country of the three – Scandinavia was regularly seen as a threat to national authenticity and the hard-won and still precarious sovereignty. This reactionary self-articulation became most obvious during the infamous clashes between the Norwegian History School – presided over by P.A. Munch and Rudolf Keyser – and primarily Danish historians concerning the ownership of the saga literature. Munch argued that Scandinavism was a Danish ruse to claim as their heritage what was truly Norwegian, and Norwegian only. A similar logic underpinned the Danish-Norwegian tug-of-war concerning such latter-day memory sites as the eighteenth-century naval hero Tordenskjold.[8] As a general point throughout the nineteenth century, a Norwegian national identity was formulated while constantly negotiating its perceived 'otherness' or 'sameness' vis-à-vis Scandinavia at large.

To sum up: in Scandinavia, national, and pan-national identity formations were entangled in multiple and complex ways. This makes clear that the pan-national movements played an intricate and hitherto underappreciated role in the development of romantic nationalism. Hopefully, my findings can be useful for the study of the other European pan-movements as well. To quote the very last sentence of my thesis: 'it is high time to re-evaluate pan-nationalism's role in European history'.

---

8 I wrote about this in an earlier issue of this journal, see Tim van Gerven, 'Whose Tordenskjold? The Fluctuating Identities of an Eighteenth-Century Naval Hero in Nineteenth-Century Cultural Nationalisms', in: *Romantik: Journal for the Study of Romanticisms* 7 (2018): 17–46.

Katrine Wonge Lohmann
(University of Copenhagen)

The Local Gothic

My project is titled 'The Local Gothic: Minerva Fiction as Nationalist Literature, 1789–1830'. The settings of Gothic novels moved from Southern Europe to Britain and became increasingly local through imitations published by the Minerva Press in the late eighteenth century. Minerva novelists repurposed British history and rewrote history in and through fiction. I claim that authors incorporated aristocratic, Protestant heroes and rational thought into stories set in familiar, historical settings. This simultaneous use and abuse of history helped establish a unified understanding of national history and identity. I started in 2018 as PhD Fellow at the University of Copenhagen, Department of English, Germanic and Romance Studies, and I will finish my project in 2022.

My main claim is that these understudied publications present a response to national fears of a Catholic past and possible invasion(s) from Continental Europe. Representing the Catholicism of the past, allowed Minerva authors to use a national past as a proxy for contemporary Catholic enemies. The representation of the past also created a distance, which allowed both readers and writers to bask in the glory of a present, enlightened Protestantism. As the Minerva Press printed fiction set in Britain, these publications give a unique insight into the British attempts to create an understanding of national unity. Dorothy Blakey compiled a list of surviving Minerva publications in 1939, and I plan to analyse roughly fifty of those works that are still in existence. This material will allow me to uncover how literature was entwined with political development. My research project has three focus areas.

The first focus area is an examination of literary conventions. The Minerva Press imitated previously published material, primarily the Radcliffe novels. I will examine a number of imitations of the Gothic author Ann Radcliffe to establish which conventions authors imitated. I also examine how Minerva authors deviated from the established conventions, and what impact this had on the Gothic genre. I claim that the conventions established by Radcliffe conveyed a fondness for Court, Church, and aristocracy; additionally the novels praised a glorified, conservative past. In terms of narrative structure, her novels also reclaimed older genres, such as the romance. These were all conservative measures responding to a cultural crisis, and the Minerva novels imitated these measures ad nauseam.

Fig. 1: Illustration for Ann Radcliffe, *The Mysteries of Udolpho*, 1793.

The second focus area is an examination of the literary depiction of landscapes. It warrants attention that the Minerva Press was the first to publish Gothic fiction set in Britain; it is, therefore, interesting to examine the scenery in these publications. I review the presentation of landscapes in a number of Minerva novels and conduct a case study of one of the popular Minerva novels: Regina Maria Roche's *The Children of the Abbey* (1796). The case study allows me to uncover how the depiction of British scenery promotes a sense of national unity, and broadening the remit of the analysis, I will determine whether promoting national unity was a Minerva trademark. I claim that values embodied by aristocratic and Protestant heroes combined with rationality became incorporated into stories set in familiar, historical, and local settings.

The third focus area is an examination of Minerva Press founder William Lane's market and marketing strategies. By examining Minerva frontispieces and in-text advertisements, I will account for the popularity of Lane's publications. I claim that Lane's success originated from three different sources: his typesetting of frontispieces, texts, and advertisements; his strategy of publishing imitations;

and his propagation of circulating libraries, which granted readers easy access to his material.

In terms of method, I combine book history with close reading of the material. I compare Gothic fiction set in imaginary Southern European settings, primarily Radcliffe's first five novels, with Minerva novels set in Britain. I examine these, both quantitatively and through a case study. Using insights from the field of book history, I examine the books as material objects by looking at the title pages, frontispieces, the typesetting of the texts and the advertisements printed at the back of the novels. In terms of addressing the anti-Catholic stance embedded in the novels, I address René Girard's scapegoat mechanism (1986). Girard discovered that a community will periodically turn to rituals whenever it is afraid. I argue that the British ritual was to engage in anti-Catholic sentiment, particularly against villains in Gothic literature. Girard's discovery allows me to examine how Gothic authors used villains as scapegoats to meet the national British fear of both Catholic Europe and Britain's own Catholic past. Girard's idea that rituals happen periodically also enables me to argue that a ritual cleansing could occur in a literary arena with each new novel. My analysis will generate a model of interpretation that shows how the repurposed history, the idealized society, the conservative nationalist ideology, and the symbolism applied by Minerva Press publications became vehicles for cultural anxiety.

My project includes both literary and historical aspects. As for the historical perspective, I take my starting point in Linda Colley's argument (1992) that a common enemy created a unity at home, and this unity was both religiously and politically motivated. This historical argument is supported by Diane Hoeveler who – from a literary perspective – argues in favour of the common enemy being Catholicism (2014). I wish to expand both these arguments and claim that the Britons found united understanding and admiration for their (constructed) past through representing this in fictional narratives. Toni Wein (2002) argues that Gothic novels reaffirm cultural values gathered from a presumed collective past. I will apply Wein's argument to the Minerva novels and thereby expand it to a new area of study. The result will be an innovative understanding of the role Gothic discourse played in establishing unity across the British nations. Colley's argument is particularly relevant as the popularity of the Minerva Press continued until 1820; hence, I argue their momentum was closely connected with Britain's outside enemy, who presented a threat until Napoleon's defeat in 1815.

Another important that theory I consider is Benedict Anderson's notion of 'imagined communities' (1983), which points to print capitalism as instrumental for building a communal consensus in the national space. Because the Minerva Press is a prime example of print capitalism, it is relevant to expand Anderson's theory. Anderson argues that imagined communities were partly the result of widely circulating publications. I argue that the widely circulating Minerva publications, which promoted a revised national(ist) history, established national unity in Britain to an extent that was unachievable for Gothic novels with foreign settings.

Review

Friederike Brun, Weltbürgerin in der Zeitenwende. Eine Biographie

By Kerstin Gräfin von Schwerin
Göttingen: Wallstein Verlag, 2019
382 pp., 41,10 Euro

Friederike Brun, nee Münter (1765–1835) was long forgotten as a writer and as a cosmopolitical figure in continental Europe 1780–1835. Even in Denmark, where her biographer Louis Bobé in 1910 was critical towards her poems, prose, and person but appreciated her connection to many famous German and Italian artists and writers. For some years now, a new interest in her life and correspondences has occurred. This well-researched and well-written biography by Kerstin Gräfin von Schwerin contributes to the renewed interest in an intellectual figure positioned between sensibility and romanticism, between Danish and German – and Italian, English, and French languages and culture. She lived in Denmark most of her life but travelled in the years 1781–1826 to Germany, Sweden, Russia, France, Switzerland, and Italy, with her parents, with husband and children, and with her friends and lovers. She published in German from the first volume of poems and the first travelogue in 1781 till the end of her life in 1836.

The renewed interest in her life is not least due to the fact that a substantial part of her many letters is now transcribed and published. The correspondence 1810–1829 with Caroline von Humboldt in *Frauen zur Goethezeit* by Ilse Foerst-Crato was published in 1975. The immense edition by Doris and Peter Walser-Wilhelm 1996–2008 *Bonstettiana* (1996–2008), consisting of more than 40 volumes of transcribed letters, diaries, and writings to and from the Swiss author Karl Viktor von Bonstetten, who, for forty years was closely connected to Friederike Brun, has been of great importance, because Friederike Brun's handwriting was and is extremely difficult to encode. The biography by Kerstin Gräfin von Schwerin builds upon the published letters and especially on the *Bonstettiana*, which is also published by Wallstein. I will conclude this review with a few reflections upon how this textual basis contributes to the portrait of Friederike Brun and what its limitation might be. But first a few remarks on the biography, the biographee and her literary works.

Fig. 1: Erik Pauelsen, Portrait of Friederike Brun with her daughter Charlotte sitting on her lap, 1789, dimensions unknown, Sophienholm.

Friederike Brun, nee Münter: Copenhagen and Europe

The first chapter in the biography concerns the childhood and adolescence of Friederike Münter. Her father was called as a minister to the German church St Petri in Copenhagen from 1765 – the year she was born in Germany. In the latter third of the eighteenth-century, Copenhagen was dominated by a German-speaking cultural elite. Friederike grew up in this open-minded milieu around the poet Klopstock and many other German intellectuals. She was tutored at home together with her older brother Friedrich by her father and private tutors. At the age of 16, she published her first small volume of poems and in 1782 a travelogue of her first journey to Germany with her parents, who introduced her to many German intellectuals and writers. From an early age, she learned to 'network' and to write in the tradition of 'Empfindsamkeit' – or sensibility. Later, she adopted elements of romanticism, inspired by Thomas Gray and Lord Byron.

The Biography

The first chapter of 17 draws a picture of the German clique in Copenhagen and Friederike Brun's autobiography *Wahrheit aus Morgenträumen* [Truth from Morning Dreams] 1824; a charming text on the first 15 years of her life that ends with her first (unhappy) love, just before her first publications. It lists many names and circumstances but does not reflect upon the personality of Friederike; nor does it reflect upon the language and style of the autobiography and its literary qualities. The autobiography was published together with the biography of Friederike Brun's youngest daughter Ida: *Idas ästhetishe Entwickelung* [Ida's Aesthetic Development] the title of which refers to Schiller's *Letters on the Aesthetic Education*. The double publication is in itself unusual, the first part reflects the upbringing of the mother to become an author, the second part reflects upon the upbringing of her daughter to become a body performer. Both parts draw a picture of idyllic childhoods, but the fact that they contradict each other is not reflected upon. Von Schwerin's interest in the factual life of Friederike Brun and her network overshadows her literary work and its aesthetic qualities. The biography depicts in the the 'Weltbürgerin' [World citizen] and cosmopolitical woman's famous connections more than the intellectual writer and woman. Why she was and even is interesting and became the talk of the town in Copenhagen, Geneva and Rome and developed strong intellectual companionship with Anna Germaine de Staël-Holstein at Coppet, and Caroline von Humboldt is hardly commented upon, just like it is not reflected why her poems and traveloques were popular and often reprinted in her time. Nevertheless, the biography offers an extremely qualified overview of persons she knew as well as where she published her bigger and many smaller works.

In the 17 chapters, Gräfin Kerstin von Schwerin closely follows the persons around Friederike Brun and her many travels and new connections in Denmark, Germany, Sweden, Russia, Switzerland, France, Italy etc. She is married, she loses a son but raises four children in the manner of Rousseau. She falls in love with the poet Friedrich von Mathisson in Lyon and with Karl Viktor von Bonstetten in Geneva. She has close connections to several outstanding women. The individual Friederike, however, does not really come to life, just as her work does not. She published five volumes of poetry and 18 volumes of travelogues, many smaller works, and two editions of letters. The list of her works covers eight pages in this book, placed after the extremely well-documented notes. Paradoxically, the double biography of Friederike Brun and Elisa von der Recke von Adelheid

Müller from 2012, comes closer to the person and her writings – even closer to the many intellectuals and artists she knew, because it documents in detail what she read, which paintings and sculptures she knew, and how she used this knowledge in her own work.

The main contribution of the biography is thus much the same as the Danish biography by Louis Bobé from 1910: to document an author by her interesting network. This documentation nevertheless is more qualified than Bobé's, not least because of the immense number of transcribed letters to and from Friederike Brun, which forms the framework. The last two chapters cover the period 1810–1836, where she lived separated from Caroline von Humboldt and Karl Viktor von Bonstetten in Copenhagen, and the conversation in their letters become less intense, just like the biography itself, except for the pages that describe her collection of poems *Lieder für Hellas* 1821 [Songs for Hellas]. Here, for the first time, we get a glimpse of a writer who insists that earnings from her poems go to the freedom fight in Greece, beyond all good taste. She bought canons for the money from her poems, canons which were sent to Greece to support the people's fight for freedom.

Kerstin Gräfin von Schwerin's biography is very solid work. For a reader who is not at home in the period 1780–1830, the many names mentioned might be overwhelming, for others it might be a help to dig deeper into the life and work of an outstanding writer. The overview is impressive, especially in the chapters that rely on *Bonstettiana*. In the last chapters, the structure is less clear, and we do not really understand what Friederike Brun was without Bonstetten – or her Father and brother Friedrich. Friederike is seen through the lens of many men and a few women and less through the lens of her many works, which are often reflections of her life, because they build on diaries and letters from her lived life and travels. This said, it is understandable that the author is not able to 'grasp' the writings of Friederike Brun, written as they are between languages, genres, styles, and periods, like Karin Hoff showed in 2003 in *Die Entdeckung der Zwischenräume* [The Discovery of the In-betweens]. I hope the biography will inspire writers who work with the period around 1800 to try to also understand the works, now that we have a qualified framework of life and connections.

Dr. Karen Klitgaard Povlsen
University of Aarhus, Denmark

About the Authors

Peter Svare Valeur is Associate Professor in Comparative Literature at the University of Bergen. He has published many articles on European Romanticism and Modernist poetry. He is a member of the research networks 'Historicizing the Aging Self, Christianity and Modernity', and 'Theories of Compilation in the 18th Century'. His PhD was titled "Romantic Figures of Old Age: Readings of Chateaubriand, Eichendorff and Wordsworth" (University of Oslo, 2013).

The University of Bergen, Department of Linguistic, Literary, & Aesthetic Studies
HF building, Sydnesplassen 7, Bergen, Norway
Peter.Valeur@uib.no

Adrian Mioc is Associate Professor of English and Comparative Literature in the Department of Languages and Cultures at the University of Western Ontario. His publications include articles on Keats, Shelley as well as American writes like Cormac McCarthy. Currently, he is working on a book project entitled Counter-Romanticism that analyzes issues of incongruity and disparity that involve prominent romantic writers. This article can be read as an illustration of such divergence.

University of Western Ontario, Department of Languages and Cultures
University College 2210, Ontario, Canada, N6A 3K7
amioc2@uwo.ca

Jørgen Huggler is Associate Professor of Philosophy at The Danish School of Education at Aarhus University. He has published on subjects such as German Idealism (Kant and Hegel), Kierkegaard, and philosophy of education. He holds a dr.phil. degree in history of ideas (Aarhus University) and a mag.art. degree in philosophy (Copenhagen University).

Aarhus University, Faculty of Arts, The Danish School of Education
Tuborgvej 164, 2400 Copenhagen NV, Denmark
johu@edu.au.dk

Andrew Kent-Marvick is a professor of art history at Southern Utah University. He holds degrees from Harvard, UCLA, and Columbia. He has published mainly on aspects of form in Symbolist art, focusing in recent years on participation by women artists in the transition to modernism in Europe. His latest research concerns Georgiana Houghton (1814–1884) and Hilma af Klint (1862–1944), two pivotal figures in the history of Western abstraction.

Southern Utah University, Department of Art and Design
351 W University Blvd. Cedar City Utah, 84720
kent-marvick@suu.edu

Louis Marvick is Professor of French at the University of Nevada, Reno. In 2004 he published Waking the Face That No One Is, a study of poetry and music in the late nineteenth century. Recent scholarly work includes articles on Alexander Scriabin, Édouard Manet, George Eliot and Gustave Moreau. His collection of uncanny short stories, Dissonant Intervals, appeared in 2016, and a series of adventures set in the eighteenth century, The Friendly Examiner, in 2020.

Department of World Languages and Literature
University of Nevada, 1664 N. Virginia Street, Reno, NV 89557
marvick@unr.edu

About the Authors

Dr Victoria Ferentinou is Assistant Professor at the University of Ioannina where she teaches art theory and history of art. She received her PhD in art history and theory from the University of Essex specialising on the oeuvre of women surrealists. She published entries in the *International Encyclopedia of Surrealism* (Bloomsbury, 2019), and is a co-editor of the anthology *Surrealism, Occultism and Politics: In Search of the Marvellous* (Routledge, 2017) and the organiser of the international symposium *Visual Ecotopias: History, Theory, Criticism* that took place in the framework of the 1st Biennale of Western Balkans (Ioannina, 2018). In 2019-2020 she was awarded a CHS-CCS Research Fellowship from the University of Harvard. Her research interests include art theoretical discourses of modernism and the avant-garde with emphasis on surrealism; the relation between word and image; feminist art theory and criticism; ecocriticism, ecoaesthetics and contemporary art.

The University of Ioannina, Department of Fine Arts & Art Sciences
P.C. 45110, Ioannina, Greece
vferen@uoi.gr

Tim van Gerven obtained his PhD in the summer of 2020 at the University of Amsterdam. His dissertation examines the interconnections between Scandinavism and the individual national movements in Denmark, Norway, and Sweden. He is currently teaching on European identity and European cultural history, also at the University of Amsterdam.

Amsterdam School for Regional, Transnational and European Studies (ARTES)
Kloveniersburgwal 48, 1012 CX Amsterdam, The Netherlands
t.w.j.vangerven@uva.nl

Katrine Wonge Lohmann is a PhD fellow at the University of Copenhagen, Department of English, Germanic and Romance Studies. Her main focus of research has been on gothic literature and the Minerva Press, and has previously taught English literature as External Lecturer at the University of Copenhagen prior to her PhD position. She is educated from the University of Copenhagen and University College London, and has published on the gothic devil, and presented on the Minerva Press and British gothic literature.

The University of Copenhagen, Department of English, Germanic and Romance Studies
Emil Holms Kanal 6, 2300 København S, Denmark
kwl@hum.ku.dk

Dr. Karen Klitgaard Povlsen is senior associate professor at The School of Culture and Communication: Media Studies, Aarhus University, Denmark. Dr. Povlsen has published extensively on mediated popular fictions, on travelogues and literature around 1800, i.e. *Northbound*, AUP 2007 and salon culture in Scandinavia, Germany, Switzerland and Italy. She has published five books, ten anthologies and around 200 articles and book chapters.

University of Aarhus, Institute for Communication and Culture.
Helsingforsgade 14, 8200 Aarhus N. Denmark.
karenk@cc.au.dk